D0553491

The Sanibel & Captiva

COOKBOOK

Sponsored by

Children's Education Center of the islands

Publication #7116

Printed in the United States of America by:

G & R Publishing Company
507 Industrial Street
Waverly, IA 50677
800-383-1679
gandr@gandrpublishing.com
http://www.cookbookprinting.com

INTRODUCTION

At the Children's Education Center of the Islands, our mission is to create - through the combination of a diversified curriculum and essential parent partnerships - a nurturing, exciting learning environment that sends forth joyful, confident, curious children who can think can for themselves, work through their problems, utilize their skills and develop their potential.

As it was in 1974 when it was founded, our preschool remains a not-for-profit, community institution, staffed by professional educators and governed by a board of volunteer parents. While tuition covers operational expenses, we rely on fund-raising and donations to pay for capital improvements and scholarships.

The Sanibel-Captiva Cookbook has been a staple among our fund-raising efforts since the first edition was published in 1981. The second edition, slightly revised, appeared in 1989. This edition, our third, represents a complete makeover from front cover to index. More than half of the nearly 400 recipes here are new and have been chosen to reflect the variety of tastes and talents at work in the islands' best restaurants and busiest home kitchens. Mixed in with the recipes are bits of Sanibel-Captiva history and trivia carried over from previous editions, plus new tips for cooks and even some words of wisdom from the little people who spice up our lives as only children can!

We hope you have fun preparing our dishes, and that you serve them to family and friends with a heaping measure of the good feeling that comes with knowing your purchase of our cookbook for yourself or for a gift will help our award-winning preschool continue its 25-year tradition in the family life of Sanibel and Captiva.

Thank you...and enjoy!
The Cookbook Committee

CHILDREN'S EDUCATION CENTER MILESTONES

1974 - - A group of Sanibel families designed a self-sustaining parent co-op and obtained use of the old Bailey's General Store, then still on the bay at the end of Bailey Road (now restored and part of the Sanibel Historical Village).

1980 - - The preschool moved to its current location on Casa Ybel Road. The Sanibel-Captiva Lions Club and the Bailey family donated five acres of land, and Casa Ybel Resort donated two guest cottages, which were moved to the site and joined together to create our main building.

1981 - - The first Sanibel-Captiva Cookbook was published as a fund-raiser by Children's Center parents.

1989 - - The second edition of the cookbook appeared.

1996 - - The National Association for the Education of Young Children awarded accreditation to our school and we joined 5 percent of child-care centers in the United States with the distinction. In part to signify our pride in this accomplishment, the school's official name was changed to the Children's *Education* Center of the Islands.

1997 - - We opened our second building, a small beach house that had been donated to the school and moved to the property several years before, and designated it for our 2-year-old classes. Many island businesses and families gave money, materials and manhours to restore the building.

1999 - - Updated from front to back, the third edition of the Sanibel-Captiva Cookbook is published.

PLEASE...AND THANK YOU!

Even though the magic words have been used countless times in connection with this cookbook project, they never seem to be enough. Of course, the recipes are the main ingredients of any cookbook, and our heartiest thanks go to each and every chef, parent, grandmom, grandpa and good friend who contributed one or more of their favorites to this third edition. As much as history, our bulging files of new contributions and our not-so-perfect memories allow, we have credited our sources whenever possible. In addition, we single out the following for generously adding their time and talents to the mix:

Third Edition
Co-chairs - - Tad Caldwell and Cindy Pierce
Artwork - - David Cutler, Mike Neal and Bob Radigan
Typists - - Mary Bondurant, Diana and Luis Perez,
Peggy Wilzbach, and Sandy Zahorchak
Proofreaders - - Tad and Jo Caldwell, Sandy Caldwell
and Mary Pulkinen
Essential others - - Sharon Chamberlain, Leslie Cook, Renae Durand,
Julie Neal and Kevin Pierce

First and Second Editions

Dorothy Andrews
Lucy Armenia
Carlene Bowen
Elinor Dormer
Mariel Goss,
  1st Edition Co-chair
Harriet Howe
Anne Kennedy
Cindy Khemkhajon
Ellie Kohlbrenner,
  2nd Edition Co-chair
Anne Kontinos
Carolyn Leonard

Eugenia Loughney,
  1st Edition Co-chair
Merri Murphy,
  2nd Edition Co-chair
Michael Murphy
Bud and Martha Ryckman
Susie Santamaria
Joe Searing
Maureen Steger
Joni Stokes
Chris Wackerman
Ron and Cherie Weaver
Sharon Webb

TABLE OF CONTENTS

WHAT'LL IT BE?

*Most Requested Favorites
from the Islands' Best Restaurants*

SANIBANANA DAIQUIRI

	Ice
1	ounce rum
1	banana
4	strawberries
	Whipped cream
	Cherry
1/2	ounce strawberry liqueur
1/2	ounce creme de bananas
4	ounce pineapple juice
1	ounce creme de coconut
	Orange, sliced

In a blender, mix 2 scoops ice, 1 ounce rum, banana, strawberries, strawberry liqueur, creme de banana, creme de coconut and pineapple juice; blend well. Garnish with whipped cream, orange slice and cherry. Makes 1 serving.

McT's Shrimphouse

Insider Island Info:

The town of Sanybel at the east end of the island was incorporated in 1833.

FRUIT SMOOTHIE

1/2	cup skim milk
1 1/2	cups ice
2	ounces fresh fruit
2	tablespoons honey

Blend all together in blender until smooth. Makes a 16-ounce drink.

The Bean

PINEAPPLE SALSA

1   can crushed pineapple
1   small can chopped jalapenos
    Fresh chopped cilantro

Mix together and serve with tortilla chips.

The Bean

Insider Island Info:

"The Narrows," the last property on Captiva to be homesteaded, was swept through by a hurricane in 1921, thus creating Redfish Pass.

SMOKED FISH DIP

1	pound smoked fish (any white fish works best)
1/2	ounce Cajun Red Fish Spice
1/2	cup green pepper, finely diced
1/2	cup red pepper, finely diced
1/2	cup onion, finely diced
1	cup Hellmann's mayonnaise

Coarsely chop fish in food processor. Transfer to mixing bowl and stir in Cajun Red Fish Spice. Add remaining ingredients and season to taste with salt and pepper. Mix well and chill well before serving with melba toast rounds.

Barnacle Phil's on Upper Captiva

LEMON HUMUS

14	ounce can garbanzo beans
	Juice of 1 lemon
1	tablespoon sesame oil
	Salt and pepper to taste
1/4	teaspoon cardamon
1	teaspoon crushed garlic

Mix all ingredients in food processor. Chill before serving with crackers or fresh, raw vegetables.

The Bean

Insider Island Info:

The first lighthouse keeper, Dudley Richardson, was appointed on November 24, 1884.

NEW ENGLAND CLAM CHOWDER

1	medium onion, chopped
	Equal amount of chopped celery
3	large potatoes, washed and cut into 1/2" cubes
3	8-ounce cans chopped clams in juice
1	8-ounce bottle clam juice
1	gallon milk
3/4	pound butter, melted
	Flour for roux
	Seasoning: white pepper, salt, whole thyme, seafood seasoning

In a large pot, put the chopped onions, celery, potatoes and all the clam juice (includes juice from chopped clams). Simmer together until the potatoes are soft. Add the clams and gallon of milk and let simmer. During this time, prepare the butter roux. Melt the butter and slowly add flour as you stir until the roux is thick, like a milkshake and smooth. Leave on the stove on a very low heat for a short while. Now it is time to season the chowder. Add a good shot of white pepper and some salt. Shake whole thyme over the chowder pot, covering at least half of the top. Add a little less seafood seasoning than thyme. Now add the roux slowly, stirring constantly until thick. Remove from heat. If the chowder gets too thick, add milk and heat again.

The Mucky Duck

COLD AVOCADO SOUP

2	cups avocado, peeled and sliced
2	cups chicken consomme
1/2	teaspoon onion juice or 1 tablespoon chopped onion
1	cup light cream
1	cup sour cream
	Salt and freshly ground pepper
	Paprika
	Chopped parsley
	Scallions, finely sliced

Blend avocado, consomme and onion juice at high speed in a blender for 5 seconds. Place cream, sour cream (a low-fat version is fine), salt and pepper in a mixing bowl. Beat until smooth and then add to the avocado mixture. Chill and serve garnished with paprika, parsley and scallions.

Sanibel Cafe

Insider Island Info:

Sanibel was officially opened to homesteading in 1888.

SANIBEL OMELET

2   extra large eggs
1   tablespoon chopped onion
6   large cooked shrimp
1   tablespoon butter

Beat eggs until light and foamy. Add onions and shrimp. Heat 1/2 teaspoon butter in 7" skillet over moderate heat. Pour egg mixture into pan. Cook until bottom is set, in the meantime, heat butter in the other 7" pan. Gently flip the omelet into the second pan. Cook until set and firm. Makes 1 serving.

NOTE: Shrimp should be fresh.

The Lighthouse

Insider Island Info:

The drawbridge and three spoil islands that make up the 3-mile-long Causeway opened to traffic in 1963. The toll was $3 per car. In 1994, 3,225,118 vehicles crossed the span from the mainland.

SHRIMP SALAD CROISSANT

3	pounds small salad shrimp, peeled and deveined
1/2	stalk celery, diced
6	hard-boiled eggs, diced
1	red onion, diced
2	cups mayonnaise
1/2	ounce Old Bay Seasoning
1	ounce Worcestershire sauce
	Garnish: 1 leaf of lettuce and 1 ounce alfalfa sprouts per serving
	Croissants

Drain salad shrimp and squeeze excess moisture out. In large mixing bowl, combine salad shrimp, celery, onions, eggs, mayonnaise, Old Bay Seasoning and Worcestershire sauce. Mix well and refrigerate. Makes 15 (4-ounce) portions.

TO FILL CROISSANT: Split croissant horizontally. Place leaf lettuce on bottom half of croissant, top with shrimp salad, alfalfa sprouts and top half of croissant. Cut in half. Makes 15 servings.

NOTE: Serve with fresh Florida fruit salad or soup.

Cap'n Al's at South Seas Plantation

STUFFED AVOCADO SALAD

2 medium avocados
2 tablespoons lemon juice
1 12-ounce package cream cheese
1 teaspoon onion juice
4 stuffed olives, chopped
2 tablespoons pecans, finely chopped
  Salt and pepper
  French dressing

Cut avocados in half lengthwise. Peel and remove seed. Scoop out 1 tablespoon pulp from each half to enlarge the seed cavity. Dip avocados in lemon juice. Blend the scooped-out avocado pulp, cream cheese, onion juice and lemon juice with a fork until smooth. Add the olives and nuts. Season with salt and pepper. Fill the avocado cavities with above mixture, then press together the matching halves and wrap in foil. Chill 3 to 4 hours.

TO SERVE: Cut avocados in slices. Place on lettuce leaves and drizzle with French dressing.

Sanibel Cafe

Insider Island Info:

The Sanibel Community Association was organized in 1926 by Curtis Perry, a visitor from Maine, who solicited funds for the building which was erected on land donated by Miss Cordie Nutt.

AVOCADO SALAD DRESSING

A slightly different taste treat best served on an assortment of greens with red and green pepper rings and chopped green onions.

1	ripe avocado
1	tablespoon lemon juice
1/2	cup light cream
1/2	cup sour cream
1	clove garlic, minced
1/8	teaspoon sugar
1/2	teaspoon salt
1	tablespoon grated onion
	Dash of cayenne pepper

Peel and mash the avocado with lemon juice. Stir light cream into sour cream and blend. Add seasonings. Stir in the avocado and chill.

Sanibel Cafe

CAPTAIN DOMINICK MANARITE'S
NO-FAIL FRESH-CATCH RECIPE

Captain Dom says, "Whatever fish you catch, take it to a restaurant and have the chef prepare it!"

If you've been out on a fishing charter, or casting from the causeway or pier or shoreline, these restaurants will gladly prepare the fruits (or the fish) of your labor:

Chadwick's
Gilligan's
The Hungry Heron
The Jacaranda
The Lazy Flamingo
R.C. Otter's
The Riviera
Sanibel Cafe
Sid's Market
Timbers
Twilight Cafe

We suggest you call the restaurant before showing up at the door with your fillets.

Insider Island Info:

Sanibel Island is 3 miles wide and 12 miles long.

SANIBEL-STYLE SWORDFISH

1	8-ounce steak of swordfish, per person (other steak-cut fish like tuna or cobia may be substituted)
1 1/2	cups key lime juice
1/2	cup white wine
1/2	cup olive oil

Whisk all liquids together and marinate fish steaks for at least 2 hours. Cook fish on the grill until done to taste.

1	shallot, thinly shaved
1	tablespoon butter
1/4	cup white wine
1/4	cup rum (white or coconut)
2	ounces Coco Lopez or other coconut cream product
1/2	cup heavy cream

Saute shallots in butter until lightly caramelized. Add rum, white wine and coconut cream; simmer for 2 minutes. Add heavy cream and simmer for 7 to 10 minutes until sauce is thick. If a thicker sauce is desired, whisk in 1 teaspoon cold butter at end of simmer time. Ladle sauce over the fish, garnish with fresh pineapple and toasted coconut shavings. Serve with fresh vegetable, rice and a crisp Chardonnay or Pinot Grigio.

Portofino at the Sanibel Inn

HORSERADISH-CRUSTED SALMON

1/4	pound butter, softened
1	egg
1	cup horseradish
1	cup fresh white bread crumbs
1	teaspoon Dijon mustard
1	teaspoon grain mustard
1	teaspoon Worcestershire
	Salt and pepper to taste
6	salmon fillets, 6 to 8 ounces each

Preheat oven to 350°. Whisk together butter and egg. Add the next 6 ingredients and mix well. Spread mixture over the top of the salmon fillets. Place on a lightly oiled baking sheet and bake for 25 minutes until golden brown. Serves 6.

Beachview Inn

GRILLED MAHI-MAHI WITH ISLAND SALSA
(JUST HOW JOCELYN LIKES IT!)

2	red peppers
2	green peppers
1	medium red onion
1	small yellow onion
1	jalapeno
6	tomatoes
1	bunch fresh cilantro
1/2	cup olive oil
1/4	cup balsamic vinegar
	Salt and pepper to taste

Dice first 6 ingredients into very small pieces and mix with chopped cilantro in a large bowl. Add olive oil and balsamic vinegar, salt and pepper. Mix by hand until all is evenly mixed. Set aside.

2	6-ounce Mahi-Mahi fillets

Brush fillets with olive oil and season with salt and pepper. Grill approximately 3 minutes on each side. Serve topped with salsa.

The Jacaranda

Insider Island Info:

The average yearly rainfall on Sanibel is 54 inches.

SEAFOOD BOCA GRANDE

6	shrimp (21 to 25 count)
6	scallops (46 to 50 count)
1	ounce chopped clams
3	ounces diced grouper
1	ounce mushrooms, sliced
1/2	ounce green onions, sliced
1/2	ounce shallots, finely diced
2	ounces butter
1/2	ounce white wine
2	ounces heavy cream
1	ounce garlic butter
2	ounces Parmesan cheese, grated
1/2	ounce lime juice
	Salt and pepper to taste
8	ounces fettuccini

Saute mushrooms, shallots, green onions with 2 ounces of butter. Add seafood; lightly cook. Add wine and simmer for 5 minutes until the liquid has reduced by 1/3; add heavy cream and bring to a boil. Turn down heat and simmer until cream reduces and thickens. Add garlic butter, lime juice and Parmesan cheese and seasonings. Serve over a bed of hot fettuccini. Makes 2 servings.

NOTE: Don't overcook seafood and don't let cream boil too long. Just simmer until the cream thickens.

Chadwick's at South Seas Plantation

SEA TROUT BELLE CHASE

4	9-ounce sea trout fillets
1	cup seasoned flour
1/4	pound butter
6	eggs, beaten
1	tablespoon chopped green onions
16	select oysters with juice
16	peeled and deveined (26 to 30 count)
	Cayenne to taste
6	medium mushrooms, quartered
1	sweet red pepper, diced
3	cups heavy cream
3	ounces vegetable oil
2	lemons
2	ounces vermouth
	Salt to taste
	Pepper to taste

TROUT: Wash trout and dust with flour. Pass through eggs and directly into hot skillet containing 3 ounces vegetable oil and 3 ounces butter. Cook until golden brown on both sides. Top with juice of 2 lemons.

SAUCE: Place in saute pan 1 ounce butter. Heat until bubbling. Saute green onions, shrimp, mushrooms and diced sweet peppers over high heat until shrimp are cooked. Add select oysters with juice, vermouth and cook until oysters are firm. Drain off liquid into saucepan and cook until liquid is reduced one half. Add cream, then cook until reduced to sauce consistency. Add salt, pepper and cayenne. Add oysters, shrimp and vegetables to sauce; simmer and serve over trout.

King's Crown at South Seas Plantation

CHARCOAL-GRILLED SHARK

1	pound butter, melted
1/4	cup minced garlic
1/4	cup minced shallots
1/4	cup chopped fresh parsley
	Shark fillets
	Fresh lemon wedges

While the coals are warming, prepare marinade. Marinate shark until the fire is ready. Make sure the grill is hot. Grill shark 3 to 4 minutes a side (depending on the thickness). Baste with marinade. Serve with plenty of fresh lemon wedges.

The Timbers

BROILED GROUPER FLORIDIAN

2	pounds grouper (4 skinless 8-ounce fillets, 1/2 to 3/4" thick)
	Water
	Dash of grated nutmeg
	Dash of black pepper
2	tablespoons vegetable oil
2	tablespoons orange juice
2	teaspoons grated orange rind

Preheat oven to 375°. Lay grouper fillets in a large, shallow, greased baking dish. Add enough water to reach halfway up the thickness of the fish. Pour the oil, orange juice, rind mixture over the fish. Sprinkle a dash of grated nutmeg and black pepper over the top. Bake at 375° for 12 to 15 minutes (depending on thickness of fillet). Do not overcook.

OTHER COOKING METHODS: The firm white flesh of the grouper makes it extremely versatile. It is excellent broiled, baked, pan fried, deep fried, poached or steamed. It may be charbroiled if put on greased foil.

The Timbers

Insider Island Info:

The Sanibel Elementary School was the first integrated public school in Lee County.

BAKED SNAPPER ALMONDINE

2   pounds red snapper (4 skinless 8-ounce
      fillets)
      Flour for dredging
1/2 cup olive oil
      Dash of pepper
1/2 cup slivered almonds
1/2 cup melted butter
      Juice of small lemon

Preheat oven to 375°. Dredge snapper fillets in flour, then saute in the olive oil until they are browned on both sides. Lay the fillets in a large baking dish and top them with the almond, butter and lemon mixture. Bake 3 to 5 minutes (or until the almonds are browned).

NOTE: Snapper is best baked, broiled, steamed or poached (whole or filleted). It is too delicate and too expensive to fry. The skin on true red snapper remains flat and tender when cooked, but the skin on other snapper tends to curl. If the skin has been scored where you buy fish, it is an indication it is not true red snapper.

The Timbers

CRAB CAKES WITH ROASTED CORN SALSA
(ALWAYS AMANDA'S FIRST CHOICE!)

ROASTED CORN SALSA:

4	ears fresh corn
1	red pepper
1	green pepper
2	tablespoons fresh cilantro, chopped
1	tomato, chopped
2	tablespoons balsamic vinegar

CRAB CAKES:

1	pint jumbo lump crab meat
1	egg
1/2	cup mayonnaise
2	teaspoons Dijon mustard
1/2	teaspoon Worcestershire
1	cup fresh white bread crumbs
1	teaspoon lemon juice
1	teaspoon Old Bay seasoning
	Dash of Tabasco sauce
	Salt and pepper to taste

ROASTED CORN SALSA: Heat oven to 350°. Roast corn for 25 to 35 minutes, and roast peppers for 1 hour. Cut corn off the cob. Peel the skin from the peppers, remove the seeds and chop into small pieces. Mix the corn and peppers together with the rest of the salsa ingredients.

CRAB CAKES: Combine ingredients and mix well. If still loose, add more bread crumbs. Pat into 3-ounce patties and flour lightly. Saute in oil or butter until golden brown. Spread corn salsa onto small plates and top with crab cakes. Serve hot. Serves 4 to 6.

Beachview Inn

J. J.'s CRAB CAKES

1	pound lump crab meat
2/3	cup mayonnaise
1/4	cup saltine cracker crumbs
1	tablespoon Old Bay seasoning
1/2	teaspoon dry mustard
1	large egg
2	tablespoons dried parsley flakes

Carefully pick all shell and cartilage from crab meat. Place crab meat and cracker crumbs in large bowl. Mix together, gently! You want to avoid breaking up the crab meat too much. With wire whisk, combine all other ingredients in separate mixing bowl until thoroughly blended. Pour this into the crab meat mixture and toss gently until all crab meat is coated. Form into eight patties and saute in butter over medium-high heat until golden brown on both sides.

The Seafood Center and Crab House

SPAGHETTINI WITH CRAB MEAT

1/2	cup extra virgin olive oil
2	cloves garlic, chopped
4	tomatoes, peeled and chopped
2	tablespoons sliced, sun-dried tomatoes
	Salt and freshly ground black pepper
2	bunches asparagus
1	pound spaghettini
8	ounces snow crab meat
1	tablespoon fresh basil, chopped
1/2	cup marscapone cheese

Heat olive oil in a heavy skillet over medium-high heat. Add garlic and cook for 2 minutes. Add chopped tomatoes and simmer for about 5 minutes. Season with salt and pepper; set side. Bring a large pot of water with a pinch of salt to boil. Drop in asparagus and cook until crisp, about 2 minutes. Remove asparagus and set aside. Return the water to a boil with a few drops of olive oil. Add the spaghettini and cook until al dente. Return the sauce to medium heat. Add the crab meat and asparagus, marscapone cheese and chopped basil. Stir gently until heated through. Serve over the cooked spaghettini. Serves 4.

The Riviera

Insider Island Info:

The Sanibel-Captiva Conservation Foundation was incorporated in 1967.

PRETZEL-CRUSTED PORK LOIN

1   cup light North American lager
1   egg
2   cups crumbs from unsalted pretzel
      nuggets
2   tablespoons finely minced scallions
1   teaspoon cracked black pepper
2   pounds pork tenderloin (in 3 to 4 pieces)

Preheat oven to 350°. Line a baking sheet with aluminum foil. Blend lager and egg until smooth and place in a long, narrow loaf pan; set aside. Crush unsalted pretzel nuggets with a rolling pin or in a food processor to make a coarse flour; set aside. Blend scallions and black pepper with pretzel crumbs in a long, shallow dish. Roll each tenderloin in the lager-egg mixture, then in pretzel crumbs and place on the baking sheet. Repeat until all meat is covered with the seasoned pretzel blend. Bake for 30 to 40 minutes or until done. Serve sliced thin with spicy mustard or maybe buttered noodles. Pair with a malty, dark lager.

Sanibel Cafe

Insider Island Info:

Sanibel Island encompasses 10,730 acres and has 11.75 miles of shoreline along the Gulf of Mexico, 3.75 miles of shoreline along San Carlos Bay and 9 miles of mangrove frontage.

FILLET OF BEEF
WITH BALSAMIC VINEGAR SAUCE
(ALA NOAH)

1	pound fillet of beef
2	tablespoons balsamic vinegar
4	tablespoons olive oil
3	sprigs rosemary
	Pinch of oregano
	Ground white pepper
	Pinch of red pepper
	Fine salt
	Coarse salt

Prepare the sauce in a saucepan by blending the balsamic vinegar, oil, rosemary, oregano, white pepper and the red pepper. Blend well over low heat using a whisk. Allow to cool. Lightly salt and pepper the fillet. Broil or grill over hot coals until the meat is rare. Cut the fillet into thin slices. Baste the slices with tepid sauce and sprinkle with a bit of coarse salt. Serves 4.

Mangia e Bevi

ROULADEN OF FLANKEN FLORENTINE

1	large flank steak (approximately 2 to 2 1/2 pounds)
1	clove fresh garlic, minced
8	ounces softened cream cheese
1/2	cup drained chopped pimento
1	cup fresh thin sliced mushrooms
1	cup drained, cooked, whole fresh spinach
4 to 5	ounces thin sliced parma ham
16 to 20	whole peeled baby onions (approximately 1 to 1 1/2" in diameter)
2	cups beef broth
2	cups red wine (medium dry to dry)
	Coarsely ground pepper
1 or 2	bay leaves
	Flour to thicken broth

Preheat oven to 350°. To butterfly flanken, lay the flank steak on the counter with length away from you. Using a long filet knife, horizontally slide the blade through the side until it almost reaches the opposite side. Carefully split the meat half and half by slowly working the knife away from you. Lay the flanken open to have 1 large piece of meat. Rub with garlic. Spread cream cheese over entire filet of meat. Sprinkle pimentos over meat. Sprinkle mushrooms over the pimentos. Lay cooked leaves of spinach over the entire surface (2 to 3 leaves thick). Lay ham slices over surface. Carefully roll meat and layered ingredients beginning with narrow end. Continue rolling and secure the end with toothpicks. Place rouladen into the center of 9x12" pan. Surround meat roll with onions. Pour broth and wine over the meat and submerge 1 or 2 bay leaves into broth. Bake in preheated 350° oven for 1 hour. Drain cooked broth from meat and onions. Set meat and onions aside to keep warm. Thicken broth into a thin gravy. Salt and pepper to taste. To serve, slice rouladen into medallions. Ladle gravy over the top, serve onions on the side. Makes 4 servings.

The Bubble Room

DUCK AU MADERE

1	5-pound duck
	Salt and pepper
	Ground thyme
	Ground mace
1	duck liver
1	teaspoon parsley
1	teaspoon shallot, minced
1	teaspoon chives
1	bay leaf
2	cloves
1/2	onion, chopped
1/2	cup chopped celery leaves
1	cup veal stock or veal gravy
1/2	cup plus 1 ounce Madeira wine
2	egg yolks
1	ounce butter

Season the duck with salt and pepper to taste and a little thyme and mace. Mash the liver with the shallots and chives and put in the cavity. Sew or skewer closed, truss and place in pot. Add the bay leaf, parsley, cloves, onion, celery leaves, veal stock and 1/2 cup Madeira. Bring to a boil, lower heat and simmer, covered, for 2 hours. Set the duck on a hot platter, discard trussing and keep hot. Remove excess fat from the pot and strain the sauce into a pan. Boil down quickly to half and remove from heat. Let cool just a bit and beat in the egg yolks, one at a time. Beat in the butter, then the 1 ounce Madeira. Pour a little sauce over the duck and serve the rest separately, hot.

Jean Paul's French Corner

BLUEBERRY SOUR CREAM PIE

2	cups sour cream
1	cup sugar
1/4	cup sifted flour
1/2	teaspoon salt
3/4	teaspoon almond extract
2	eggs
1	9-inch unbaked graham cracker crust
2	cups canned, ready to use blueberry pie filling
1/2	cup whipped cream (can substitute Cool Whip)

Preheat oven to 375°. Combine sour cream, sugar, flour, salt, almond extract and eggs; beat well. Pour into pie shell; bake for 30 minutes. Spread filling over hot pie; chill. Whip cream; spread over pie. Served chilled. Makes 6 servings.

NOTE: We find it better at home or restaurant to keep whipped cream or Cool Whip separate and put it on individual pie pieces before serving.

Timmy's Nook

Insider Island Info:

The Sanibel Shell Fair originated at the Matthews Hotel where visitors were encouraged to display their collections. In 1927 it became a community affair.

MUCKY DUCK BROWNIES

1/2	cup butter
4	ounces unsweetened chocolate
4	egg whites, at room temperature
1/4	teaspoon salt
2	cups sugar
1	teaspoon vanilla
1	cup sifted all-purpose flour
1	cup chopped walnuts or pecans

Grease a 9x13" baking pan and preheat oven to 350°. Melt butter and unsweetened chocolate in double boiler or microwave oven. Cool this mixture. Using a hand mixer, beat the egg whites and salt in glass bowl until foamy. Add sugar and vanilla gradually and continue beating until well creamed. With a few swift strokes, combine the cooled chocolate mixture with the eggs and sugar. Do this manually. Before the mixture becomes uniform in color, fold in, again by hand, the flour. Before the flour is uniformly colored, gently stir in the chopped nuts. Bake for about 25 minutes. Cut when cool. Garnish with ice cream, hot fudge and whipped cream or an icing.

NOTE FROM THE RECIPE COLLECTORS: We did some sweet talking to get this recipe from Kathy Mayeron. These are the ULTIMATE BROWNIES!

The Mucky Duck

MAD HATTER MUD PIE

1	cup chopped almonds or walnuts
6	ounces melted butter
30	Oreo cookies
3/4	gallon chocolate ice cream
3/4	gallon vanilla ice cream
3/4	gallon strawberry ice cream

GARNISH:
2	ounces hot fudge
	Whipped cream
	Handful of slivered toasted almonds

Mince Oreos and almonds together. Add melted butter to make a crust. Layer bottom of pan with mixture and freeze for 1 hour. Soften ice cream a little and layer vanilla, chocolate and strawberry on top of crust; freeze. Cut to serve, then top with hot fudge, whipped cream and sprinkling of slivered almonds.

The Mad Hatter

Insider Island Info:

There are 22.6 miles of public bike paths on Sanibel.

KEY LIME PIE

4	large eggs, separated
3 1/2	ounces Key lime juice
1	14-ounce can sweetened condensed milk
1	9-inch graham cracker crust

Mix together egg yolks, condensed milk and lime juice. Stir until thickened. In another bowl, whip the egg whites to a full peak. Add the frothy egg whites to the egg yolks, milk and juice mixture and mix thoroughly with your hands. Pour the filling into the pie shell and freeze until solid. Pie is sliced and served frozen (about 3 hours). Makes 6 to 8 servings.

NOTE: Be sure to mix the egg whites with your hands so they don't lose the air. We use Borden's condensed milk.

The Mucky Duck

Insider Island Info:

Sanibel temperatures average between 45 and 80 degrees during the winter months and 70 and 90 degrees during the summer.

RED VELVET CAKE

CAKE:
2 1/2	cups self-rising flour
1	cup buttermilk
1 1/2	cups vegetable oil
1	teaspoon baking soda
1	teaspoon vanilla extract
1/4	cup red food coloring (yes, 1/4 cup!)
1 1/2	cups sugar
1	teaspoon unsweetened cocoa powder
1	teaspoon white vinegar
2	large eggs

FROSTING:
1 1/2	sticks butter, softened
1	1-pound box confectioners' sugar
10	ounces cream cheese, softened
1 1/2	cups chopped pecans

CAKE: Preheat oven to 350°. Mix together all cake ingredients with an electric mixer. Spray three 9" round cake pans with nonstick coating. Pour the batter equally into the 3 pans and bake for 45 minutes. Test for doneness by inserting a toothpick into the center of the cake. It is done when the toothpick comes out clean.

FROSTING: Mix cream cheese and butter until smooth. Add sugar and mix. When smooth and well mixed, add pecans and frost the cake with equal amounts of frosting for each layer.

The Bubble Room

TROPICAL CARROT CAKE

CAKE:

2	cups oil
2 3/4	cups sugar
4	eggs
1	tablespoon vanilla
1 1/3	cups crushed pineapple
1 1/3	cups grated coconut
1 1/3	cups grated carrots (mush)
1 1/3	cups chopped walnuts
3 1/3	cups flour
1	tablespoon baking soda
	Pinch of salt
2	teaspoons cinnamon

ICING:

1	pound butter
3	cups powdered sugar
2	teaspoons vanilla
	Juice of 1 lemon
3	pounds cream cheese

CAKE: Preheat oven to 360°. Mix oil, sugar, vanilla and eggs. Add fruit and nuts; mix for 30 seconds. Slowly add all dry ingredients. Don't over mix. Pour batter into three 9" greased and floured cake pans. Bake for 50 to 60 minutes.

ICING: Cream butter, sugar, vanilla and lemon. Slowly add cream cheese until well blended. Spread icing evenly between layers. Serves 12 to 18.

'Tween Waters Inn

PEANUT BUTTER PIE

1	cup peanut butter
8	ounces cream cheese
1	cup sugar
2	tablespoons melted butter
1	cup heavy whipping cream
1	tablespoon vanilla
1	cup chocolate fudge sauce
1	chocolate pie crust

Blend peanut butter, cream cheese, sugar and melted butter until creamy. Whip the heavy cream until fluffy. Fold into peanut butter mixture. Fold into chocolate pie crust. You'll have some leftover; put into pastry bag for decorating the top of the pie. Spread chocolate fudge sauce over pie. Using pastry bag, add a ring of pie filling to the outside edge and a dollop in the center. Chill well before serving.

The Seafood Center and Crab House

Insider Island Info:

The average elevation on Sanibel is 4 feet above sea level. The maximum elevation found on the island is 13 feet above sea level.

WE'LL DRINK TO THAT!

*Refreshing Beverages
from Fruit Smoothies to Spirited Cocktails*

HONEY DEW-KIWI SMOOTHIE

2	cups seeded ripe honey dew melon chunks
1	Granny Smith apple, cored and cut into chunks
1	kiwi fruit, peeled and cut into chunks
1	cup ice cubes
3 to 4	tablespoons sugar
1	tablespoon fresh lime juice

Combine all ingredients in a blender or food processor and puree until smooth. Yields 2 servings.

MANGO-ORANGE SMOOTHIE

1	1-pound ripe mango, peeled, pitted and cut into chunks
1	cup each orange juice and low-fat vanilla ice cream
1	cup ice cubes
1/2	teaspoon vanilla extract

Combine ingredients into a blender and puree until smooth. Yields 2 servings.

Kitchen Tid-Bit:

To cut a mango, hold the fruit on end and cut down alongside the flat side of the broad seed. Do this three or four times until you've sliced all around the seed. Take a slice and score the flesh diagonally, making diagonal cuts every 3/4 inch. Be careful not to cut through the rind. Give the slice a quarter turn and continue scoring the flesh, cutting it into a diamond-shaped pattern. Pick up the mango slice and, using your thumbs, push the skin up, pressing the fruit outward (sort of like you're turning a tennis ball inside out). The flesh opens to reveal chunks of mango that can easily be lifted from the peel with the edge of a spoon.

BANANA SMOOTHIE

1	ripe banana
1/2	cup nonfat vanilla yogurt
1	tablespoon sugar
1	tablespoon banana liqueur
1	cup crushed ice
1	teaspoon fresh lime juice
	Lime wedge or banana slice, for garnish

Combine all ingredients (except garnish) and puree until smooth.
Serve in a large glass, garnished with lime wedge or banana slice.

CITRUS YOGURT SHAKE

1	large Florida white or ruby red grapefruit, sectioned and with pith removed
1/4	cup frozen Florida orange juice concentrate, thawed
1	Florida valencia or honeybell orange, sectioned and with pith removed
2	cups nonfat yogurt
1/4	cup fresh strawberries, quartered
1	banana, quartered
1	teaspoon vanilla
	Other fruit may be added, including: pineapple, persimmons, peaches, raspberries

Combine all ingredients into a blender or food processor and puree for 1 minute. Serve chilled. Makes 1 (8-ounce) serving.

THAI FRUIT SHAKE

1	cup diced watermelon
1	ripe banana, peeled and diced
1	cup diced fresh pineapple
1	tablespoon fresh lime juice
2	tablespoons sugar
2	tablespoons sweetened condensed milk
2	cups crushed ice

Toss all ingredients in a blender or food processor and puree until smooth. Adjust flavoring to taste.

Quotable Kid:

Some nights it's not worth fighting
over who gets the top bunk.
Matthew, 10

MANGO MUSCLE

1/2   cup chopped mango
1/2   cup chopped papaya
2   teaspoons nonfat vanilla yogurt
1   cup crushed ice

Combine all ingredients in a blender or food processor. Puree for 1 minute. Serve chilled. Yields 1 (16-ounce) serving.

PEANUT BUTTER PROTEIN POWER

1/2	ripe medium banana
1	teaspoon peanut butter
1/2	cup nonfat frozen vanilla yogurt
3/4	cup crushed ice
1/4	cup water

Combine all ingredients in a blender or food processor. Puree for 1 minute. Serve chilled. Yields 1 (16-ounce) serving

FRUIT JUICE COOLER

2	6 1/2-ounce bottles sparkling mineral water, chilled
1	12-ounce can peach nectar, chilled
1/2	cup unsweetened orange juice, chilled
1/4	cup unsweetened grapefruit juice, chilled
2	tablespoons lemon juice, chilled

Pour all ingredients into a large pitcher and stir well. Serve on ice. Yields 4 cups.

CRANBERRY COOL-DOWN

1	ripe medium banana, halved
8	medium fresh or frozen strawberries
1	cup cranberry juice
1/2	cup crushed ice

Combine all ingredients in a blender or food processor. Puree for 1 minute. Yields 1 (16-ounce) serving.

LEMONADE SYRUP

2	cups sugar
2 1/2	cups water
1	cup mint leaves
2	oranges (grate peel of 1 orange)
6	lemons
1	glass container

Combine sugar and water; cook for 5 minutes, cool slightly and then pour cooked sugar water over 1 cup mint leaves in bowl. Add to bowl, juice of 2 oranges, 6 lemons and grated peel of 1 orange and cover mixture. Steep for 1 hour (as if preparing tea). Stir into glass container, cover and keep in refrigerator. Makes 1 quart syrup.

NOTE: Allow 1/2 cup lemonade base for each glass of water.

Mrs. Neal Bowen
Wife of Sanibel's first city attorney

SUN TEA WITH LEMON AND ORANGE

3/4   gallon cold water
10   decaffeinated tea bags
1   large lemon, sliced
1/2   cup orange juice
    Mint leaves for garnish

Fill one gallon jar 3/4 full of cold water. Add tea bags. Place outside in sun for 3 to 4 hours. When ready to serve, add lemon and orange juice. Fill large glass with ice cubes and pour tea over ice. Garnish with fresh mint.

Nancy Gerhard

SPICED ICE TEA

8	tea bags
24	whole cloves
1/3	cup lemon juice
	Large handful washed mint leaves
2	cups sugar
1	tray ice cubes
6 to 8	cups water (cold)

In a saucepan, put 8 tea bags, a large handful of washed mint leaves and 24 whole cloves into cold water and bring to a boil, simmer 10 minutes. In a large pitcher, put 2 cups sugar, add hot tea, stir to dissolve sugar and add 1/3 cup lemon juice. Add a tray or more of ice cubes. Set aside; refrigerate. Serve in tall glasses with ice cubes. Delicious. Makes a lot.

Kay McRae

Quotable Kid:

Puppies still have bad breath,
even after eating a Tic-Tac.
Stephen, 4

WHITE SANGRIA

1	gallon good Chablis
	Juice of 1 lemon
	Juice of 1 orange
	Juice of 1 lime
	Sugar to taste
8 to 10	sprigs fresh mint
8 to 10	strawberries

Combine all of these ingredients with slices of lemon, orange and lime. Chill for a full day before serving. Do not dilute with soda. May be strained, but not necessary.

Porter Goss
First mayor of Sanibel
and U. S. Congressman

RED WINE SANGRIA

1	tablespoon sugar
2	tablespoons orange liqueur
2	tablespoons brandy
1	bottle dry red wine
1	lemon, thinly sliced
1	lime, thinly sliced
1	orange, thinly sliced
1	bottle (1 litre) 7-Up

Combine all of the ingredients except the 7-Up. Cover and refrigerate for at least 2 hours. Just before serving, add the 7-Up and lots of ice. You may want to add more sugar or 7-Up depending on your taste.

HOT SPICED WINE PUNCH

1	quart apple juice
1	quart cranberry juice
1/2	cup lemon juice
2	quarts rose wine
1	quart water
2	cups sugar
4	cinnamon sticks
12	whole cloves
	Peel of 1 lemon, cut in strips

Combine cranberry juice, apple juice, water, sugar, cinnamon sticks, cloves and lemon peel in saucepan. Bring to a boil. Stir until the sugar has dissolved. Simmer, uncovered, 15 minutes. Add wine and lemon juice. Heat, but do not boil. Serve in punch bowl. Garnish with lemon slices. Makes about 40 servings.

NOTE: Be sure punch bowl is capable of holding hot punch. Great punch for the holidays!

Thomas Loughney

SANIBEL WAVE

6   ounces gin
     Juice of 1 lemon
10   leaves fresh mint
3   ounces frozen limeade
     Juice of 1 lime

Fill blender with crushed ice. Add all ingredients. Blend well. Don't add water to limeade. Last one in is all dry!

Gloria Avis Johnson

NERVE TONIC

1 1/2   ounces gin or vodka
        Ice
        Unsweetened pink grapefruit juice
        Pinch of salt

Fill an 8-ounce glass with ice and add the gin or vodka. Add enough juice to fill the glass. Add the pinch of salt. Stir.

Gloria Avis Johnson

Kitchen Tid-Bit:

Champagne, the celebration beverage, is best served very cold. In the average refrigerator this takes a couple of hours. We have a way to take the temperature down in just 20 minutes: Fill an ice bucket half full of ice cubes. Pour in several cups of cold water and add 4 tablespoons of salt. Plunge the bottle of bubbly into the bucket, then add water and ice almost to the top. Let sit for 20 minutes.

(For more modest celebrations, this method works equally well with beer and white wine.)

LIME LIQUEUR

2	dozen fresh limes
6	cloves
6	cups 80 proof vodka
	Green food dye
1/2	teaspoon ground cinnamon
2	pounds white sugar
2	cups water

Wash limes. Cut each lime into 5 or 6 slices. Combine with cinnamon, cloves, vodka, water and white sugar. Shake until sugar dissolves. Cover. Set in cool place for 2 weeks. Strain through fine sieve and leave aside to clear. Decant and pour clear liqueur into bottles.

Grace Shepherd

KAHLUA

2   ounces instant coffee
4   cups sugar
     Vodka
2   cups boiling water
     Vanilla bean

Dissolve coffee in boiling water. Add sugar. Stir well and cool. Cut vanilla bean into quarters. Put 2 pieces in each of 2-quart bottles. Pour 1 cup vodka into each bottle. Add sugar mixture (half in each bottle). Then fill the rest of bottles with vodka. Cap tightly and hide for 30 days!

Mary Aleck

MINT JULEP

Bourbon
Sugar
Cracked ice
Fresh mint

Chill julep cups or glasses in refrigerator. Before serving, put 1 teaspoon sugar or 2 small sugar cubes in bottom of cup (or glasses). Add a splash of bourbon to dissolve sugar and 2 or 3 fresh mint leaves. Muddle (crush and mix together). Fill cup (glass) with cracked ice and fill with bourbon. Put in refrigerator if not served immediately. Must be served frosty! Add a sprig of mint.

Porter Goss
First mayor of Sanibel
and U. S. Congressman

SYLLABUB

3	quarts cream
1	quart milk
1 1/2	cups bourbon
3	cups sugar
1 1/2	cups rum

Mix cream and milk, stir in sugar, add rum and bourbon. Place in a deep pan and churn with syllabub churn (you may use an egg whip in case you don't have a syllabub churn). Lift off foam when it is firm enough not to break when touched. All ingredients should be well chilled before mixing and the syllabub should be served immediately so that it will not fall. It does not "stand" for long. It should be ladled from a bowl into tall glasses and served with a spoon. It is usually accompanied with a sweet cake.

Quotable Kid:

It's hard to unlearn a bad word.
Collin, 5

HOT BUTTERED RUM

1	pound butter
2	pounds brown sugar
3	beaten eggs
1	teaspoon cinnamon
1	teaspoon ground clove
1	teaspoon allspice
1	teaspoon nutmeg

Melt butter and add spices. Pour over brown sugar, let cool. Add beaten eggs. Beat with mixer approximately 30 minutes. Batter will keep indefinitely in covered container in refrigerator. To serve, add 1 tablespoon butter, 1 jigger rum to a mug of boiling water. Stir with cinnamon sticks.

Linda Bjerke

STEPHEN'S FAMOUS MOJITO
(A CLASSIC CUBAN DRINK)

1	teaspoon sugar
1 1/2	ounces light rum
4 to 5	fresh mint leaves
	Crushed ice
	7-Up to taste
1	stick sugarcane for garnish
1	slice lime for garnish

Place the sugar, rum and mint leaves in a cocktail shaker and shake vigorously until sugar dissolves. Fill a tall rocks glass with crushed ice and pour the cocktail over the ice. Add 7-Up and stir gently. Garnish with the sugarcane stick and lime.

Stephen Day
(via Danny Mellman, via Joseph Dolce)

RUM PUNCH

1	can frozen orange juice
6	3-ounce cans water
6	ounces grenadine
1 1/2	ounces Mount Gay rum
	Ice cubes
1	can frozen pineapple juice
6	ounces orange Curacao
1 1/2	ounces Meyers dark rum
1	teaspoon lime juice
	7-Up or bitter lemon

Put orange juice, pineapple juice, water, Curacao and grenadine into a 2-quart container. To make a tall cool drink, put 3 ounces of this mix into a tall frosted glass and add the rum, lime juice, ice cubes and 7-Up or bitter lemon to each drink.

Jane Valtin

KARI'S DADDY'S MANGO DAIQUIRI

2	ripe mangoes, peeled
1 1/2	ounces light rum
1	tablespoon lime juice
3 to 4	tablespoons sugar (optional)

In blender, combine ingredients with crushed ice. Blend and serve two.

David Fowler

THE LAURENTIANS'
ABSOLUTE BEST BLOODY CAESAR
(PERFECTED BY LAURA'S DADDY)

2	ounces vodka
6	ounces Clamato® juice
1/2	teaspoon horseradish
5	shakes Worcestershire sauce
1/2	of a lemon
5	shakes Tabasco
	Freshly ground black pepper
	Celery salt
1	celery stalk

Sweep the lemon wedge over the top of the glass and dip the glass in celery salt. Mix all the rest of the ingredients in a cocktail shaker and pour the mixture into the glass full of ice. Squeeze the remaining lemon in the glass and garnish with a fresh celery stalk. Yield: Serves one very happy customer.

NOTE: To make a bloody Caesar it is essential to use only Clamato juice.

John Chenciner

Quotable Kid:

Twelve is a lot older than eight.
Britt, 8

CAPTIVA CONDIMENTS AND SANIBEL STARTERS

Relishes, Dips and Appetizers Galore

LIME MARMALADE

6	key limes
2 1/2	cups water
	Sure-Jell
2	lemons or 2/3 tablespoon juice of lemon
1/8	teaspoon soda
6 1/2	cups sugar

Remove skins of limes in quarters. Lay flat and shave off and discard about half of white part. Slice rind very fine. Add 2 1/2 cups water and 1/8 teaspoon soda. Simmer, covered, 20 minutes. Chop peeled fruit and add pulp and juice to cooked rind. Simmer, covered, 10 minutes. Add water, if necessary, to make 4 cups rind and pulp mixture. Mix Sure-Jell with fruit. Place over high heat and stir until mixture comes to hard boil. At once add 6 1/2 cups sugar. Bring to full rolling boil. Boil hard 1 minute, stirring constantly. Remove from heat. Stir and skim for 7 minutes to cool slightly and prevent floating fruit. Add green coloring. Pour into jelly glasses.

Grace Shepherd
With thanks to Ann Krausse

MANGO HAMBURGER RELISH

1	quart green mangoes, peeled and chopped
2	large onions, chopped
6	green peppers, chopped
2	large hot peppers, chopped
1	tablespoon salt
1	tablespoon mustard seed
1	tablespoon celery seed
1 1/2	cups sugar, or to taste
1	cup vinegar

Mix all chopped vegetables and fruit. Then add the other ingredients. Cook for 10 minutes. Let stand overnight. Next day, cook until thick. Put in sterilized jars and seal.

Patsy Simmons

JOCELYN'S MOM'S
SPICY CUCUMBER MELON RELISH

2	tablespoons sugar
2	tablespoons fresh lime juice
2	teaspoons chopped fresh cilantro
1/4 to 1/2	teaspoon crushed red pepper flakes
1/8	teaspoon salt
1/8	teaspoon coarsely ground black pepper
1	cup diced seeded cucumber
1/2	cup diced seeded watermelon
1/2	cup diced honeydew
1/4	cup chopped red onion

Combine sugar, lime juice, cilantro, red pepper flakes, salt and pepper. Stir until sugar dissolves. Just before serving, add remaining ingredients. Toss gently to combine. Serve with grilled seafood, chicken or beef.

Lee Harder

ZUCCHINI RELISH

12	cups sliced squash
4	cups sliced onions
5	tablespoons salt
2 1/2	cups vinegar
5	cups sugar
1	tablespoon dry mustard
3/4	teaspoon cornstarch
1 1/2	teaspoons celery seed
1/2	teaspoon black pepper
3/4	teaspoon turmeric
2	teaspoons cinnamon
1	red sweet pepper, ground in food processor
1	green pepper, ground in food processor

Mix first 3 ingredients together. Let stand overnight. Rinse with cold water and drain. Mix remaining ingredients and cook until mixture starts to thicken. Bring to a boil. Add squash and onions; cook slowly for 30 minutes. Can while relish is hot.

Dot Lantz

HORSERADISH CREAM
(A GREAT ACCOMPANIMENT FOR SMOKED FISH, BOILED SHRIMP OR ANY RAW OR COOKED SEAFOOD, STEAKS AND ROAST BEEF)

2	cups nonfat plain yogurt
1	tablespoon white horseradish or finely grated fresh root
1	clove garlic, minced
1	shallot, minced
1	tablespoon minced fresh chives
1	teaspoon Dijon mustard
1	teaspoon fresh lemon juice
	Salt and freshly ground black pepper

Line a colander with cheesecloth and let yogurt drain through it for 2 hours (or drain it in a yogurt funnel). Add remaining ingredients to the yogurt and stir. Adjust the seasoning to taste. The sauce is meant to be very spicy.

Cindy Pierce

TOASTED COCONUT CHIPS

1	average size coconut
1	teaspoon salt
1	tablespoon sugar

Take the meat of an average sized coconut. Leave the brown skin on. Cut into thin strips. A potato peeler is excellent for this task. Put in large bowl and toss with 1 level teaspoon of sugar and 1 teaspoon of salt. Spread on cookie sheet and put in 250° oven. Stir every 20 minutes until completely dried out and a golden brown. This will take between 1 and 2 hours, depending on the thickness of the chips. Keep in tight tin. Even then you may have to recrisp in oven before serving. They absorb moisture quicker than you think.

Mary Aleck

GLAZED PECANS

2	egg whites
1	cup sugar
	Pinch of salt
1 1/2	pounds pecans
1/4	pound butter

Beat egg whites until stiff and add sugar and pinch of salt. Beat until not sugary. Add pecans and mix well. Melt butter in 9x13" pan. Spread nuts into pan, coating with the melted butter. Bake at 325° for 30 minutes, turning every 10 minutes to recoat with the butter. Spread out on foil to cool.

Lois Gobrecht

Quotable Kid:

It's only fun to play school
when you're the teacher.
Katie, 5

PEKING PECANS

1 pound pecans
6 tablespoons butter
2 tablespoons soy sauce
Salt
Freshly ground pepper

In shallow pan at 350°, toast pecans with butter for 10 minutes. Cool a little. Add salt or crazy salt, pepper and soy sauce. Mix and drain on brown paper bag.

Patsy Simmons

ZESTY CRACKERS

1	pound Cheddar cheese, grated
3	cups all-purpose flour
1	cup (2 sticks) butter, room temperature
1	teaspoon salt
1/4	teaspoon cayenne pepper
1	cup chopped pecans

Beat first 5 ingredients with electric mixer until well combined. Mix in pecans. Divide dough into thirds. Form each into smooth 1 1/2" diameter log on sheet of waxed paper. Wrap tightly. Refrigerate at least 1 hour to firm. (Can be prepared ahead and refrigerated 3 days or frozen for several months. Thaw in refrigerator before continuing.) Preheat oven to 325°. Remove paper from dough. Cut dough into 1/4" thick slices. Arrange 1 1/2" apart on baking sheets. Bake until golden brown. Transfer to paper towels and cool completely. Store in airtight container.

GREAT GUACAMOLE

3	ripe avocados
1	teaspoon lemon juice
1/2	cup onion, chopped
1	cup sour cream
1 1/2	teaspoons Worcestershire sauce

Mash avocados in bowl. Stir in lemon juice. Add remaining ingredients, mixing well by hand or on high speed with an electric mixer for 2 minutes.

Cindy Sitton

CREAM CHEESE GUACAMOLE

1	ripe medium sized avocado
2	3-ounce packages cream cheese
2	tablespoons lemon juice
3 to 4	tablespoons LaVictoria Salso Ranchera
	(add more for hotter guacamole)

Soften cream cheese. Mash avocado, add to cream cheese. Mix lemon juice and hot sauce with above ingredients.

NOTE: Delicious in omelets with cheese and sprouts; in salads, sandwiches, dips or alone.

Carol Dorais

JEZEBEL

1   large jar pineapple preserves
2   small jars apple jelly
1   small can dry mustard
1   jar horseradish
1   tablespoon sour cream
     Cream cheese

Mix preserves, jelly, dry mustard and sour cream; blend well. Pour over cream cheese and serve with crackers.

Jane Morgan

WIL'S MAMA'S SENSATIONAL SALSA

3	14 1/2-ounce cans chopped tomatoes
1	10-ounce can Ro-Tel chopped tomatoes with green chilies
1	4 1/2-ounce can chopped green chilies
1	bunch green onions, chopped
4	cloves fresh garlic, chopped
2 (or more)	jalapeno peppers, chopped
1/4	cup cilantro, finely chopped
1	teaspoon cumin
1/2	teaspoon chili powder
2	tablespoons lime juice
	Salt and pepper to taste

Mix all ingredients in bowl and refrigerate overnight.

Cindy Sitton

BEST BLACK BEAN SALSA

1	15-ounce can black beans, drained and rinsed
1	11-ounce can yellow corn
2	medium tomatoes, diced
1	red bell pepper, diced
1	green bell pepper, diced
1/2	cup diced red onion
2 to 3	fresh jalapeno peppers, sliced thin
1/3	cup cilantro, finely chopped

MARINADE:

1/3	cup fresh lime juice
1/4	cup olive oil
1	teaspoon salt
1/2	teaspoon cumin
1/2	teaspoon cayenne pepper

Combine beans, corn, tomatoes, bell peppers, onion, hot peppers and cilantro. In separate bowl or in jar, combine marinade ingredients and stir or shake until mixed. Pour over salsa and stir to combine. Let marinate several hours to combine flavors before using.

Cindy Sitton

MULLET PATÉ

1	8-ounce package cream cheese, softened
2	smoked mullet filets (can use smoked amberjack)
2	stalks celery, minced fine
1/2	red pepper, minced fine
1/2	cup red onion, minced fine
2	tablespoons mayonnaise
	Dash of lemon juice and hot sauce
	Season to taste with salt and pepper

Remove meat from fish, carefully checking to make certain that bones are not present. Add all other ingredients to the fish and refrigerate for a minimum of 2 hours. Serve with fresh bagel chips or toast points.

Quotable Kid:

Never ask your 3-year-old sister
to hold a tomato.
Allen, 7

CRAB MEAT PIZZA ON A PLATE

12	ounces cream cheese
2	tablespoons Worcestershire sauce
1	tablespoon lemon juice
2	tablespoons mayonnaise
	Dash of garlic powder
	Small grated onion
1/2	bottle chili sauce
6	ounces flaked crab meat
	Chopped parsley

Mix together the first 6 ingredients. Spread on pizza pan, pie plate or round plate. Spread with the 1/2 bottle of chili sauce (more if needed). Top with flaked crab meat (fresh crab meat can also be used). Sprinkle with chopped parsley. Chill for several hours or overnight. Serve as spread on crackers.

Lois Mast

CRAB MEAT PUFFS

1	6-ounce package frozen crab meat, thawed, drained, cartilage removed and chopped
6	ounces cream cheese, softened
1/2	teaspoon salt
1/4	teaspoon garlic powder
40	won ton skins
1	egg, slightly beaten
	Vegetable oil

Mix the crab meat, cream cheese, salt and garlic powder until well blended. Brush the top of a won ton skin with the egg. Place a heaping teaspoonful of the crab mixture in the center of the won ton skin. Top with another won ton skin and press the edges to seal. Brush a dab of egg on the center of each side of the puff. Make a pleat on each side, pressing to seal. Repeat with the remaining won ton skins.

NOTE: Keep completed puffs and the unused won ton skins covered with a damp towel to keep them from drying out.

Heat vegetable oil (1 1/2" deep) in wok to 350°. Fry 4 or 5 puffs at a time until golden brown, turning 2 or 3 times (about 2 minutes). Drain on paper towels. Serve with your favorite dips (mine are plum sauce and Chinese mustard). Makes 20 appetizers.

TIP: Prepared crab meat puffs can be frozen for up to 6 weeks. Just before serving, heat frozen puffs, uncovered, in a 400° oven for 10 minutes (until hot). Drain on paper towels.

HOT CRAB SPREAD

3	large packages cream cheese, room temperature
2	crushed garlic cloves
2	teaspoons prepared mustard
2	teaspoons powdered sugar
2	cans crab meat
1/4	cup mayonnaise
1/4	cup white wine
1	teaspoon onion juice
1	teaspoon creamy horseradish
	Salt to taste

Whip together and heat in a double boiler or chafing dish. Serve with your favorite crackers.

Mrs. Leland Moree, Jr.

BONNIE'S PARADISE ARTICHOKE AND CRAB DIP

1	8-ounce package cream cheese
1	cup mayonnaise
1	14- to 15-ounce can artichoke hearts
1	6-ounce can crab meat
1/2	cup grated Parmesan cheese

Blend all ingredients, pour into an 8x8" pan. Bake at 350° for 15 to 20 minutes until golden brown. Serve with crackers, tortilla chips, pita bread or your other favorite dippers.

Mary Bondurant

SHRIMP SEA ISLAND

2 1/2	pounds shrimp, cleaned and cooked
5	mild white onions
1	cup olive oil
3/4	cup cider vinegar
1	small bottle capers, liquid too
	Salt, Tabasco, sugar and Worcestershire sauce to taste

Marinate all ingredients in large bowl for 48 hours. Drain and serve in pretty dish. If you find that olive oil has too strong a taste, mix with vegetable oil.

Helen Sierier

Quotable Kid:

The best place to be
when you're sad
is Grandma's lap.
Morgan, 8

GRILLED SHRIMP AND POTATO FOCACCIA

1	recipe fresh pizza dough (this may be purchased frozen)
1/4	cup olive oil
2	white potatoes, washed, peeled and sliced very thin
1/2	of a red onion, cut in half and sliced thin
1/2	cup fresh grated Parmesan cheese
1	teaspoon fresh chopped herbs, if desired
	Kosher salt and ground pepper
1/4 to 1/2	pound grilled shrimp (brush with melted butter, lemon juice, salt and pepper before grilling)

Grease a cookie sheet with olive oil and dust with cornmeal. Spread pizza dough to cover the bottom of the sheet and set aside. Cook onions in 1 teaspoon of olive oil until they are translucent. Brush top of dough with olive oil and spread onions on top. Next layer potatoes, herbs and grated cheese on the dough; sprinkle with olive oil. Season with salt and pepper to taste. Bake for 45 minutes to 1 hour at 350° or until focaccia is lightly browned. Cut into squares and top with warm grilled shrimp. Serve warm.

SUN-DRIED TOMATO AND BEAN DIP

3	ounces sun-dried tomatoes
1/3	cup fresh basil leaves
2	tablespoons balsamic vinegar
1	tablespoon olive oil
2	tablespoons Italian-style tomato paste
1	15-ounce can cannelli beans, drained
1	clove garlic, minced
	Salt and pepper to taste
2	peppers (red, green or yellow), seeded and chopped

Combine all ingredients in blender or food processor and process to desired consistency. Serve with your favorite dippers. (Italian bread sticks are great.)

Mary Bondurant

TEX-MEX TACO DIP

1	can chopped, drained green chilies
1	can refried beans
2	large avocados
1	tablespoon lemon juice
1	cup sour cream
1/2	cup taco sauce
1 1/2	cups grated sharp Cheddar cheese
1	cup chopped green scallions
2	large tomatoes, chopped and drained
1	6-ounce can pitted black olives, sliced
	Taco chips

Stir green chilies into refried beans. Mash avocados with lemon juice. Blend sour cream with taco sauce. Layer all ingredients on a large serving dish (approximately 13 to 14" diameter). If possible, let chill for a couple of hours before serving. Serve with plain taco chips.

Sheryl Pharr,
Donna Sublett

IAN'S FAVORITE MEXICALI CORN DIP

2	cans Green Giant Mexicali corn, drained
1	bunch green onions, sliced (save some for top)
1	cup mayonnaise
1	cup sour cream
2	cups grated Cheddar cheese
2 to 3	jalapenos, chopped (optional)

Mix everything together and sprinkle a few green onions on top.
Serve as a spread on crackers (we like Triscuits or Wheat Thins).

Barbara Molnar

TACO PLATTER SPREAD

1   8-ounce package cream cheese
1   package taco mix
1   cup sour cream
    Sweet onion, minced

GARNISH:
Green pepper, chopped
Chopped lettuce
Diced tomatoes
Grated cheese
Chopped black olives

Blend cream cheese with taco mix seasonings. Add sour cream. Mix and spread on platter. Top with chopped green pepper, lettuce, diced tomatoes, grated cheese, black olives and minced sweet onion. Serve with tortilla chips.

Helen Pierce

Quotable Kid:

Your room gets smaller as you get bigger.
Brynn, 12

RYAN'S MOM'S
BAKED CREAM CHEESE APPETIZER

1	4-ounce package refrigerated crescent dinner rolls
1	8-ounce package cream cheese
1/2	teaspoon dill weed
1	egg yolk, beaten

Remove dough from package and roll onto a lightly floured surface. Press seams together to form a 12x4" rectangle. Sprinkle 1/4 teaspoon of the dill onto the cream cheese and lightly press it in. With the dill-side down, place cream cheese in the center of the dough. Toss remaining dill onto the cream cheese. Bring sides of dough together, encasing the cream cheese and seal the edges by pressing them together. Place on a lightly greased cookie sheet and brush with egg yolk. Bake for 15 to 18 minutes at 350° until lightly browned. Serve with crackers and apple slices.

Mary Beth Greenplate

CUSTARD HORS D'OEUVRES

1   cup chopped onions
1   cup shredded sharp Cheddar cheese
1   cup mayonnaise
     Doritos

Mix onions, cheese and mayonnaise together. Bake slowly at 275° to 300° for 45 minutes so mayonnaise does not separate. Excellent plain, but may add other ingredients as below. Use Doritos to dip. Makes 6 servings as appetizers. Recipe can be doubled.

MAY ADD: Herbs, crab, shrimp, ham, bacon or your favorite vegetable to mix before baking for variety.

Debby Pavelka

"STERLING" ARTICHOKE DIP

8	ounces artichoke hearts, drained (not marinated)
1	cup mayonnaise
1	cup grated Parmesan cheese
1	4-ounce can mild green chilies, chopped
1/2	clove garlic, crushed

Mix ingredients. Pour into a baking dish and bake at 375° for 10 to 15 minutes, or until heated through. Serve with crackers.

Sharon Chamberlain

CAROLINA PIMENTO CHEESE SPREAD

2	8-ounce packages extra sharp cheese
1	8-ounce package sharp cheese
1	4- to 6-ounce jar diced pimento
1	12-ounce can evaporated milk
4	tablespoons mayonnaise
1	tablespoon coarse ground black pepper
1/2	teaspoon Tabasco sauce
1/2	teaspoon Worcestershire sauce
1	teaspoon sugar

Grate cheeses. Mix remaining ingredients with cheeses and refrigerate. Should be made one day in advance so all milk can be absorbed into the cheeses.

Cindy Sitton

KIMBERLY'S EASY CLAM DIP

1   can minced clams
1   8-ounce package cream cheese
1   small onion, diced

Blend together cream cheese and diced onion. Drain juice from clams; set aside. Add minced clams to cream cheese mixture and stir in clam juice until desired consistency is obtained.

Mary Beth Greenplate

Quotable Kid:

Don't say "Last one is a rotten egg"
unless you're sure there's a slow kid behind you.
Carly, 5

TARRAGON PARTY DIP

1   cup mayonnaise
3   hard cooked eggs, chopped
2   tablespoons green onions, finely chopped
2   tablespoons fresh parsley, finely
      chopped
2   tablespoons capers (optional)
2   teaspoons Dijon mustard
1   tablespoon tarragon vinegar
1   tablespoon fresh lemon juice
1   clove garlic, crushed
1   teaspoon prepared horseradish
2   teaspoons fresh tarragon or 1 teaspoon
      dried, crumbled

Combine all ingredients thoroughly. Cover and refrigerate for several hours or overnight. Serve with crackers, shrimp or raw vegetables.

Marge Clark

GOURGERE PUFFS

1/2	cup hot water
1/8	teaspoon salt
1/2	cup all-purpose flour
	Dash of cayenne pepper
1/2	cup (2 ounces) shredded natural Swiss cheese
1/4	cup butter or margarine
1/8	teaspoon sugar
3/4	teaspoon dry mustard
2	eggs

In a small saucepan, combine water, butter or margarine, salt and sugar. Beat until butter melts and mixture boils. Vigorously stir in flour, dry mustard and cayenne all at once. Stir over medium heat until mixture leaves sides of pan. Remove from heat; by hand, stir in eggs, one at a time, until blended. Stir in cheese. Drop from teaspoon onto greased baking sheet. Bake in 450° oven for 10 minutes. Reduce heat to 375° and bake 15 minutes, until puffed and golden. Turn off oven and let puffs remain inside 3 minutes more. Serve hot. Makes 20 appetizers.

NOTE: Can be mixed ahead and baked when needed.

Lucy Armenia

HOT BLUE CHEESE PUFFS

5 1/2	cups all-purpose flour
1	pound butter or margarine
1	cup cold water
1	tablespoon vinegar
1	pound blue cheese
2 or 3	egg yolks

1. Divide butter or margarine into 5 parts. Butter should be chilled, but not too hard to work into the flour.
2. Work 1/5 of the butter into the flour as for pie crust.
3. Add vinegar and cold water and knead well into a smooth dough that slides easily on the bread board and in hands.
4. Chill in refrigerator (approximately 30 minutes).
5. Sprinkle bread board with flour and place chilled dough on board. Roll out dough to a square approximately 16".
6. Place remainder of butter on top of dough and fold over butter, folding ends to meet in middle. Dough will now be 4 layers thick.
7. Roll out dough again and refold as before. Chill 10 minutes. Repeat procedure 2 more times, then chill thoroughly in refrigerator, approximately 2 hours. It is then ready for rolling.
8. Divide dough into 4 sections, cut each into 12 pieces.
9. Roll each piece to size of a tea cup, 3 to 4" round. Place about a teaspoon of blue cheese on half of the round, roll ends over to secure blue cheese.
10. Place on ungreased baking sheet.
11. Brush with slightly beaten egg yolk.
12. Bake at 325° for 30 to 40 minutes.

Makes 48 puffs or 24 servings. Serve hot out of oven with a bit of parsley for garnish.

Evelyn Pearson

GRUYERE-ONION TART

2	tablespoons butter
3	large onions, thinly sliced
1	prepared refrigerated pie crust
2	cups Gruyere cheese, grated
1	tablespoon all-purpose flour
1	teaspoon fresh thyme, chopped
1/2	teaspoon salt
1/4	teaspoon nutmeg
1/4	teaspoon white pepper
2	eggs, room temperature
1/2	cup half and half

In a large skillet, over medium heat, melt butter. Cook onions until very soft and golden, stirring occasionally. Meanwhile, preheat oven to 425°. Gently press crust onto bottom and sides of an 11" tart pan with removable bottom. Arrange Gruyere cheese evenly over the crust; sprinkle with flour, thyme, salt, pepper and nutmeg. Fork lightly to combine. Smooth top to make an even layer.

In a small bowl, whisk together eggs and half and half. Pour evenly over onion and cheese mixture. Place tart on a cookie sheet and bake for 10 minutes. Reduce heat to 375° and bake an additional 30 minutes or until filling is puffy and set. Cool slightly before serving.

Nancy Gerhard

ZUCCHINI BISCUITS

3	cups thinly sliced zucchini, unpared
1/2	cup finely chopped onions
2	tablespoons parsley, chopped
1/2	teaspoon salt
1	garlic clove, chopped
4	eggs, slightly beaten
1	cup Bisquick baking mix
1/2	cup grated Parmesan cheese
1/2	teaspoon oregano
	Dash of pepper
1/2	cup vegetable oil

Grease a 13x9x2" pan. Mix all the ingredients. Spread into pan. Bake at 350° for 35 minutes or until golden brown. Cut into pieces about 2x1". Makes 4 dozen.

Norma Leas

Quotable Kid:

Crawling still gets you there.
Natalie, 3

SPANOKOPITA

2	10-ounce packages chopped spinach, well drained
1	bunch spring onions, chopped
1/4	pound feta cheese
1	pound cottage cheese
2	eggs, beaten
	Salt and pepper to taste
	Fresh dill or 1/4 teaspoon dried dill
	Filo dough
	Melted butter

Mix first seven ingredients and let stand. On a clean countertop, place a sheet of filo. Brush it with butter. Place a second sheet on top of the first and brush it with butter. With a sharp knife, cut the filo sheets into 5 equal pieces, widthwise. Place a heaping teaspoon of filling near the edge of each of the strips. Carefully roll the filo to cover the filling, making sure to fold in the sides. Bake in 375° oven for 20 minutes.

NOTE: Filo dough is a thin pastry dough, found in Middle Eastern food stores, gourmet stores or the frozen food section of some supermarkets.

Eugenia Kontinos Loughney
Co-chair, 1st edition
Sanibel-Captiva Cookbook

TIROPITA

Beat 2 eggs
Add pepper to taste
Add enough feta and cottage cheese to
   make a thick paste
Filo dough
Melted butter

On a clean countertop, place a sheet of filo. Brush it with butter. Place a second sheet on top of the first and brush with butter. With a sharp knife, cut the filo sheets into 5 equal pieces, widthwise. Place a heaping teaspoon of filling near the edge of each of the strips. Carefully fold the sheet diagonally to form a triangle. Bake in 375° oven for 20 minutes.

NOTE: Filo is a thin pastry dough found in Middle Eastern food stores, gourmet stores or frozen food section of some supermarkets.

Eugenia Kontinos Loughney
Co-chair, 1st edition
Sanibel-Captiva Cookbook

ELIZABETH'S
EXTRA-SPECIAL SPINACH PIE

3/4	pound Muenster cheese, thinly sliced
3	10-ounce packages chopped spinach, thawed and drained
1	cup feta cheese, crumbled
3	eggs, beaten
1	small onion, chopped
1/3	cup Parmesan cheese
1/2	teaspoon dill weed
1/4	teaspoon black pepper
	Paprika

Line a 10" pie plate with overlapping slices of Muenster. Cover bottom and sides of plate. Combine spinach with feta cheese, eggs, onions, Parmesan cheese, dill weed and pepper. Place in pie plate. Shake paprika over top. Bake, uncovered, in 350° oven for 1 hour. Let stand 5 minutes before serving.

Cindy Sitton

BENCHMARK
CHEDDAR CHEESE BALL

2	cups (8 ounces) shredded sharp Cheddar cheese
6	3-ounce packages cream cheese, softened
1	medium onion, grated
3	tablespoons Worcestershire sauce
2	drops hot sauce
1/2 to 1	clove garlic, minced
1	cup chopped pecans

Combine all ingredients except pecans; mix well. Chill overnight. Shape into a ball, roll in pecans.

Sherry Anderson

BLUE CHEESE BALL FOR BRAD

2	8-ounce packages cream cheese
4	ounces blue cheese, crumbled
8	ounces sharp Cheddar cheese, grated
1	tablespoon Worcestershire sauce
1/4	teaspoon cayenne pepper
1/2	teaspoon seasoned salt
1/4	teaspoon garlic powder
2	tablespoons grated onion
	Chopped pecans

Using electric mixer, beat softened cheeses until blended. Add remaining ingredients and beat until blended. Form into 2 balls and refrigerate until hardened. Roll in chopped pecans. Better if made one day in advance.

Cindy Sitton

FETA CHEESE BALL

2	tablespoons parsley leaves, chopped
5	large radishes, thinly sliced
1	small garlic clove
2	medium green onions, chopped
1	8-ounce package cream cheese, at room temperature, cut in 4 pieces
4	ounces feta cheese, room temperature, rinsed and cut in half
1	tablespoon sour cream
1	teaspoon dried dill weed
1/2	teaspoon dried oregano
1/4	teaspoon freshly ground pepper
	Salt (optional)

Set aside the parsley and radishes to be used later as garnish. In a blender, chop fine the remaining ingredients. Line a dish with plastic wrap. Empty blender ingredients onto dish, mold into ball. Refrigerate until firm. Decorate firm cheese ball by covering it with radishes and parsley.

Patsy Simmons

WORLD'S BEST BEEF BALL

1	4 1/2-ounce jar dried beef
1	2 1/4-ounce jar dried beef
2	8-ounce packages cream cheese
3	green onions, chopped fine
1/2	teaspoon garlic powder
2	teaspoons Worcestershire sauce

Shred dried beef in blender or food processor. Reserve small amount of shredded beef to roll ball in. Combine shredded beef, onions, garlic powder and Worcestershire sauce. Add softened cream cheese. Form into ball and roll in reserved beef. Better if made one day in advance.

Cindy Sitton

Quotable Kid:

A pencil without an eraser
might just as well be a pen.
Kirsten, 7

HOT BEAN DIP

1	pound ground beef
1	can refried beans
1	can kidney beans, mashed
1	jar taco sauce
1	tablespoon chili powder
1	teaspoon cumin
	Jalapeno pepper, cut up
1	cup Cheddar cheese, grated
1/2	cup onion, chopped
1/2	cup black olives, sliced

Brown and drain ground beef. Add refried beans, kidney beans, taco sauce, chili powder, cumin and jalapeno pepper. Mix all ingredients and place in an ovenproof serving dish. Top with Cheddar cheese, onion and black olives. Cover and bake at 350° for 20 minutes. Serve hot with nacho chips.

Sharon Webb

HANKIE PANKIES

1	pound ground round
1	pound Bob Evans hot sausage
1	pound Velveeta cheese, diced
1	tablespoon Worcestershire sauce
1	teaspoon oregano
1/2	teaspoon garlic salt
1/2	teaspoon salt
	Dash of pepper

Brown meats, drain and add diced cheese. Stir until melted. Add remaining ingredients. Spread on party rye bread. Place on cookie sheet under broiler until bubbly.

NOTE: Can be frozen on cookie sheets for later use.

Janet Cramer

IRISH MEATBALLS

1	pound ground beef
1/2	cup instant mashed potatoes
1/4	cup Irish whiskey
1	medium onion, finely chopped
1	teaspoon thyme
1	teaspoon oregano
1/2	cup milk
1	egg
1	teaspoon dry mustard
1	teaspoon salt
1/2	teaspoon pepper
1/4	cup finely chopped parsley
1	3-ounce package cream cheese with chives

Mix all ingredients except cream cheese together. Refrigerate, covered, for 1 hour. Preheat oven to 400°. Form meat mixture into balls about the size of walnuts. Place on baking sheet and bake for 20 minutes. Remove from heat and drain; cool and chill. Slice meatballs in half, spread with cream cheese, about 1/4" thick. Place meatballs back together and refrigerate until needed. Serve cold. Makes 30 meatballs.

Thomas Loughney

MANHATTAN MEATBALLS

1 1/2	pounds ground beef
1	teaspoon salt
1/4	teaspoon pepper
1	beaten egg
1	tablespoon catsup
1	slice white bread, trim crust
2	tablespoons oil for sauté

SAUCE:

1	small onion, chopped
1/2	teaspoon garlic salt
1/4	teaspoon salt
1/4	teaspoon crushed oregano
1	teaspoon flour
1	beef bouillon cube
1	cup boiling water
	Dash of bitters
1	teaspoon mustard
2	jiggers bourbon
1	jigger sweet vermouth

Mix meatball ingredients together and form about 50 tiny meatballs. Heat 2 tablespoons oil, saute meatballs on both sides. Remove meatballs; add salt, onion, oregano, garlic salt and fry until onions are brown. Blend in the flour and mix. Add bouillon cube to boiling water and add to sauce. Mix well. Add whiskey, bitters and vermouth; mix until it thickens, about 1 minute. Don't overcook. Place meatballs in the sauce, simmer about 10 minutes. Put in refrigerator overnight and warm the next day.

Irene Culnan

RUMAKI

1/3	cup soy sauce
2	tablespoons vinegar
12	chicken livers
18	bacon slices, cut in half
3	tablespoons brown sugar
1/2	teaspoon salt
1	8 1/4-ounce can water chestnuts or 1 can chunk pineapple

Make a marinade of soy sauce, vinegar, brown sugar and salt. Cut each chicken liver in thirds. Cut chestnuts in 1/4" slices. Wrap a piece of liver and a slice of chestnut in half strip of bacon. Fasten with toothpicks. Marinate 4 hours or more. Place on rack in 400° oven for 20 minutes. Serve warm.

NOTE: May substitute 1 chunk pineapple for water chestnuts.

Kay Schultz

SAUSAGE BALLS

1	pound bulk sausage
1/3	cup bread crumbs
1/8	teaspoon Italian seasoning
1	tablespoon soy sauce
1	tablespoon vinegar
1	egg
1/4	teaspoon ground sage
1/2	cup chili sauce
2	tablespoons brown sugar
1/2	cup water

Combine sausage, egg, bread crumbs, sage and Italian seasoning; mix thoroughly. Shape into small balls, brown on all sides in skillet; drain on paper towels. Remove fat from skillet and add chili sauce, soy sauce, brown sugar, vinegar and water; stir well. Add meatballs to skillet, cover and simmer for 30 minutes. Refrigerate until ready to serve, then reheat and serve with cocktail picks.

Anna Marie McCord

OUR DAILY BREAD

Muffins, Loaves and Rolls
for Breakfast and Beyond

COFFEE CAKE MUFFINS

1/4	cup firmly packed light brown sugar
1/4	cup chopped pecans
1	teaspoon ground cinnamon
1 1/2	cups all-purpose flour
2	teaspoons baking powder
1/4	teaspoon baking soda
1/2	cup sugar
1/4	teaspoon salt
1	large egg
3/4	cup milk
1/3	cup vegetable oil

Mix together the brown sugar, pecans and cinnamon; set aside. In a large bowl, add and stir flour, baking powder, baking soda, sugar and salt. Make an indentation in the center of the mixture with a spoon. Blend together egg, milk and oil; pour into the indentation. Stir just until ingredients are all moistened. Line a muffin tin with paper baking cups and spoon 1 tablespoon batter into each cup. Top with half of the brown sugar mixture. Spoon remaining batter evenly among the cups and top with remaining brown sugar. Bake for 22 to 24 minutes at 400° or until lightly browned. Yields 1 dozen.

AUNT ANNA'S COFFEECAKE

2	cups flour
2	teaspoons baking powder
1 1/2	cups sugar
3/4	cup butter
2	eggs
3/4	cup milk
1	teaspoon vanilla

Sift dry ingredients; mix with butter. Take out 3/4 cup for topping. Beat eggs well with beater, combine with milk and vanilla. Beat until creamy. Butter and flour 9x13" pan. Pour in batter, cover with topping, sprinkle with cinnamon. Bake at 350° for 50 to 60 minutes. This is a thin cake, but delicious.

Gloria Kasten

Quotable Kid:

If you want a kitten,
start out by asking for a horse.
Caitlin, 5

SOUR CREAM COFFEECAKE

1/4	pound butter
2	eggs
2	cups flour
1	teaspoon baking soda
1	cup sugar
1	cup sour cream
1	teaspoon baking powder
1	teaspoon vanilla

TOPPING:
2	tablespoons flour
4	tablespoons sugar
	Chopped nuts
2	tablespoons butter
1/2	teaspoon cinnamon

Cream sugar and butter; add eggs, add dry ingredients. Alternately add sour cream. Add vanilla. Mix ingredients for crumb topping and sprinkle on top. Bake at 350° for 45 minutes in an angel food pan.

Georgia Hermphill,
Lois Cassavell

THE TWINS' FAVORITE BANANA BREAD

3	very ripe bananas, mashed
1	cup sugar
2	eggs, beaten
4	tablespoons melted butter
1 1/2	cups flour
1/4	teaspoon salt
1	teaspoon baking soda
	Dash of vanilla extract

In a mixing bowl, stir together bananas, sugar and butter. Add flour, salt and baking soda; mix well. Mix in a dash of vanilla. Pour batter into a lightly greased bread tin and bake at 350° for 45 minutes or until an inserted toothpick comes out clean. May add walnuts if desired.

Jo Caldwell

BONANZA BREAD MUFFINS

1	cup sifted all-purpose flour
1/2	teaspoon salt
2	teaspoons baking powder
1/3	cup wheat germ
1/4	cup chopped walnuts
1/2	cup raisins
1/2	cup vegetable oil
1/2	cup orange juice
1/3	cup chopped dried apricots
1	cup whole wheat flour
1/2	teaspoon baking soda
2/3	cup nonfat dry milk powder
1/2	cup firmly packed brown sugar
1/2	cup chopped pecans
3	eggs
1/2	cup molasses
2	medium bananas, mashed

Combine flours, salt, soda, baking powder, dry milk, wheat germ, sugar, nuts and raisins in a large bowl; blend thoroughly with fork. Whirl eggs in blender until foamy. Add oil, molasses, orange juice, bananas, whirl after each addition. Add apricots and whirl just to chop coarsely. Pour mixture into bowl with dry ingredients and stir just until flour is moistened. Line muffin tin with cupcake papers and bake at 350° for 20 minutes.

NOTE: You can substitute raw chopped apples, grated carrot, applesauce, fresh ground apricots, peaches, pears or even grated zucchini instead of bananas.

Dorothy Andrews

STEVIE'S FAVORITE
BLUEBERRY POPPYSEED BRUNCH CAKE

CAKE:
2/3	cup sugar
1/2	cup butter
2	teaspoons grated lemon peel
1	egg
1 1/2	cups unbleached flour
2	tablespoons poppy seeds
1/2	teaspoon baking soda
	Dash of salt
1/2	cup sour cream

Preheat oven to 350°. Cream together the sugar and butter. Add lemon peel and egg. Combine flour, poppyseeds, baking soda and salt. Add alternately with sour cream to above mixture. Spray sides and bottom of 10" springform pan. Spread batter over bottom and about 1" up sides of pan.

FILLING:
2	cups fresh or frozen blueberries
1/3	cup sugar
2	teaspoons flour
1/4	teaspoon nutmeg

Mix together filling ingredients and spoon over batter. Bake for 45 to 55 minutes or until golden brown. Cool slightly. Remove sides of pan and drizzle with glaze made of:

1/3	cup powdered sugar
2	teaspoons lemon juice

Maxine Fisher

LOVELY LEMON BLUEBERRY BREAD

BREAD:

6	tablespoons butter, room temperature
1	cup sugar
2	large eggs
1/2	cup milk
1 1/2	cups flour
1	teaspoon baking powder
1/4	teaspoon salt
2	teaspoons grated lemon peel
1 1/2	cups blueberries, fresh or frozen

Preheat oven to 325°. Cream sugar and butter. Mix in eggs and milk. Add all other bread ingredients except blueberries. When well mixed, gently fold in blueberries. Bake in well-greased loaf pan for 1 hour and 15 minutes. Cool 30 minutes.

SAUCE:

1/3	cup sugar
3	tablespoons lemon juice

In small saucepan, over medium heat, cook 1/3 cup sugar with 3 tablespoons lemon juice until sugar is melted. Poke holes in loaf with fork or skewer and drizzle sauce over bread.

FOUR-STAR CALAMONDIN BREAD

15	calamondins
2/3	cup sugar
1	cup margarine or butter
1 1/2	cups brown sugar
4	eggs
4	cups flour
3	teaspoons soda
2	teaspoons salt
1/2	teaspoon ground cloves
1	teaspoon cinnamon
1 1/2	cups coarsely chopped walnuts

Wash fruit; cut in quarters and seed. Puree in blender with 2/3 cup sugar (should measure about 2 1/4 cups). Preheat oven to 350°. Sift flour, salt, soda and spices. Cream margarine or butter with brown sugar. Add eggs, beating after each addition. Add dry ingredients alternately with calamondin mixture. Add nuts. Pour into 2 greased and floured pans (3 1/2x5x8") lined with waxed paper (including sides). Bake at 350° until firm to the touch, about 40 to 60 minutes (I have found it takes close to an hour).

Ann Krausse

COCONUT BREAD

2	cups all-purpose flour
1 1/4	cups sugar
1	teaspoon salt
4	teaspoons baking powder
1	cup milk
2	tablespoons butter
1	egg, beaten
2	teaspoons vanilla
3	cups grated, fresh coconut with brown skin

Combine flour, sugar, salt and baking powder; mix well. Melt butter and add to milk. Stir in the beaten egg and vanilla. Add to the flour mixture along with coconut; mix well. Pour into buttered loaf pan (9x5") and let rise for 45 minutes. Bake at 350° for 60 to 75 minutes.

NOTE: One large coconut gives an ample 3 cups of shredded coconut. To extract the meat, put drained coconut in 350° oven for 15 minutes, no longer. Give it a few taps with a hammer as soon as it is cool enough to handle; the nut should break open, making the meat easy to remove.

Jeannie Bond

COCONUT GROVE
CRANBERRY-ORANGE BREAD

2	cups all-purpose flour
3/4	cup sugar
1 1/2	teaspoons baking powder
1	teaspoon salt
1/2	teaspoon baking soda
1	cup cranberries
1/2	cup walnuts
1	grated orange peel
1	egg
3/4	cup orange juice
2	tablespoons salad oil

Sift together the dry ingredients; stir in nuts, cranberries and orange peel. Combine egg, orange juice and salad oil; add to dry ingredients, stirring just until moistened. Pour into 8 1/2x4 1/2x2 1/2" loaf pan. Bake in 350° oven for 50 minutes or until done. Remove from pan and cool.

Anne Kontinos

LIME OR LEMON BREAD

6	tablespoons softened shortening
1	cup sugar
2	eggs
	Grated rind of 1 lemon or lime
1	tablespoon lime or lemon juice
1 1/2	cups unsifted flour (all-purpose)
1/4	teaspoon salt
1	teaspoon baking powder
1/2	cup milk

Dissolve 1/2 cup of sugar in juice from lemon or lime to pour over hot bread. Cream shortening and sugar. Add eggs and beat. Add grated rind of lemon (or lime) and lime or lemon juice. Alternate dry ingredients with milk. Pour into greased and floured regular loaf pan. Bake at 350° for 50 to 60 minutes. As soon as baking is completed, add juice of lime or lemon in which sugar has been dissolved. Spoon over hot loaf. Cool 10 minutes. Remove from pans.

NOTE: Chopped nuts can be added to make this even better. You may also use 3 small loaf pans (if so, bake for 30 to 40 minutes at the same heat).

Martha Ryckman
First director of the Children's Center

ORANGE MUFFINS

1	tablespoon butter
3	tablespoons sugar
1	beaten egg
2	cups flour
1/2	teaspoon salt
1	cup milk
2	teaspoons baking powder
	Orange juice
12	sugar cubes

Cream butter and sugar. Add next 5 ingredients and mix. Bake in 350° oven about 25 minutes. Just before putting in the oven, dip a sugar cube in orange juice and press in each muffin. Makes 12 muffins.

Dorothy Schnelle

Quotable Kid:

If you don't like the birthday girl,
don't go to the party.
Allison, 6

ORANGE, LEMON, DATE AND NUT BREAD

2	cups flour
1/2	teaspoon soda
1	egg
2	tablespoons strained lemon juice
2	tablespoons melted butter
1/2	teaspoon salt
3/4	cup broken California walnut meats
3/4	cup strained orange juice
1	tablespoon grated orange rind
1/4	teaspoon grated lemon rind
3/4	cup chopped dates

Sift flour with soda, salt, broken walnut meats and dates. Combine 1 well beaten egg, orange juice, lemon juice, grated orange rind, grated lemon rind and melted butter. Add to dry ingredients and stir until just mixed. Turn into greased 4 1/2x8 1/2" loaf pan, lined with waxed paper. Bake in moderate oven (350°) for 75 minutes. Wrapped in foil and refrigerated, this will keep well for 2 weeks.

Molly Wolfe

PUMPKIN BREAD

1 1/2	cups sugar
2	eggs
1 2/3	cups flour, sifted
1/2	teaspoon cloves
1/4	teaspoon baking powder
1/2	teaspoon nutmeg
1/2	cup nuts
1/2	cup salad oil
1	cup pumpkin
1	teaspoon baking soda
3/4	teaspoon salt
1/2	teaspoon cinnamon
1/2	cup currants

Mix together all ingredients. Pour into greased loaf pan. Bake at 350° for 1 hour.

Faye Wollenberg

EASY SPINACH-CORN MUFFINS

1   10-ounce package frozen chopped spinach
2   5.7-ounce packages fat-free corn muffin mix

Microwave frozen spinach according to package directions. Drain; set aside. Prepare corn muffin batter according to package directions. Blend cooked spinach into the muffin batter. Spray a muffin tin with nonstick spray and spoon batter evenly among the muffin cups. Bake according to muffin directions, until an inserted toothpick comes out clean. This may require a few extra minutes of baking time.

MEXICAN CORN BREAD

1	cup yellow cornmeal
1/2	teaspoon salt
1/2	teaspoon soda
1/3	cup liquid shortening
1	cup cream style corn
2	eggs, beaten
2/3	cup buttermilk or cream
1	cup grated cheese (American, Cheddar or Jack)
1	cup green chili peppers

Mix all ingredients except cheese and peppers. Pour half of mixture in greased 9x9" pan. Sprinkle with cheese and peppers. Cover with other half of mixture. Bake at 275° for 30 to 40 minutes.

NOTE: Penny Rogers submitted a similar recipe, adding 1 small chopped onion to the batter.

Betty Bray

ZUCCHINI BREAD

2	cups unpeeled, grated zucchini
2	cups sugar
1	teaspoon vanilla
1 1/2	teaspoons baking soda
1 1/2	teaspoons baking powder
1	cup raisins
4	eggs
1	cup oil
3 1/2	cups flour
1 1/2	teaspoons salt
1	teaspoon cinnamon
1	cup chopped walnuts

Mix the eggs, sugar, oil and vanilla. Add dry ingredients slowly. Add zucchini, raisins and walnuts until all mixed. Lightly grease 2 loaf pans or 5 small loaf pans with oil. Bake at 350° for 55 minutes. After baking, let stand 10 minutes before turning out of pans.

Norma Leas

CHEESY PULL-AWAY BREAD

1/4	cup grated Parmesan cheese
3	tablespoons sesame seeds
1	teaspoon dried basil
1	25-ounce package frozen roll dough, thawed
3	tablespoons butter or margarine, melted

Mix together first 3 ingredients and scatter one third of it into a buttered 12-cup bundt pan. Put half of the roll dough in the pan. Pour half of the melted butter on top and sprinkle with one half of the remaining cheese. Repeat the layering with remaining dough, butter and cheese mixture. Place the bundt pan in a warm location free from drafts and let dough rise until doubled in size (approximately 2 hours). Bake for 30 minutes at 350°. If bread is becoming too brown, cover the pan with aluminum foil after 20 minutes. Loosen bread from side of pan with a knife when it is done and invert onto a serving plate. Yields 1 loaf.

NOTE: One may also make a Cinnamon Pull-Away Bread, by substituting a cinnamon mixture for the cheese mixture. Follow all other directions, but allow to cool in pan for 5 minutes before inverting onto serving plate.

CINNAMON MIXTURE:

1/2	cup chopped pecans
1/2	cup sugar
1 1/2	teaspoons ground cinnamon

KATE'S BRUSCHETTA

1	cup pitted ripe olives
2	teaspoons balsamic vinegar
2	cloves garlic, minced
1	teaspoon capers
1	teaspoon olive oil
2	medium red or yellow tomatoes, chopped
1/3	cup green onion, thinly sliced
1	tablespoon olive oil
1	tablespoon Italian seasoning
1/8	teaspoon pepper
1	loaf French bread
2	tablespoons olive oil
1/2	cup grated Parmesan cheese

FOR OLIVE PASTE: Combine olives, balsamic vinegar, garlic, capers and 1 teaspoon olive oil in a blender container or food processor bowl. Cover and blend until a nearly smooth paste forms, stopping and pushing the mixture down the sides as necessary. The mixture can be stored in an airtight container and chilled up to 2 days.

FOR TOMATO TOPPING: Stir together chopped tomatoes, green onion, 1 tablespoon olive oil, Italian seasonings and pepper in a small bowl. The mixture can be stored in an airtight container and chilled for up to 2 days.

FOR TOASTS: Preheat oven to 425°. Cut bread into 1/2" thick slices. Brush both sides of each slice lightly using 2 tablespoons of olive oil. Arrange slices in a single layer on an ungreased baking sheet. Bake for about 5 minutes or until light brown, turning once. Cooled toasts can be stored in an airtight container up to 2 days.

TO ASSEMBLE: Spread each piece of toast with a thin layer of olive paste, then 2 teaspoons of tomato topping. Sprinkle with Parmesan cheese. Arrange slices on an ungreased baking sheet. Bake in a 425° oven for 2 to 3 minutes or until cheese starts to melt and toppings are heated through. Serve warm. Makes approximately 24 pieces.

Sharon Chamberlain

COUNTRY FRENCH HERB FLATBREAD

1	10-ounce Pillsbury refrigerated pizza crust
4 1/2	teaspoons olive oil
2	teaspoons dried herbs de Provence (or mix 1/2 teaspoon each: thyme, marjoram, rosemary and basil)
6	oil-packed sun-dried tomatoes, drained and chopped
1/3	cup chevre (goat cheese), softened
2	eggs
	Dash of pepper

Heat oven to 400°. Spray 13x9" pan with cooking spray. Unroll dough, place on sprayed pan. Starting at the center, press dough with hands. With fingers, make indentations over the surface of dough. Brush with 3 teaspoons of olive oil. Sprinkle with herbs and tomatoes. In a medium bowl, combine cheese, eggs, remaining oil and remaining herbs. With a wire whisk, mix well. Pour evenly over tomatoes, spread carefully. Bake at 400° for 15 to 20 minutes until edges are golden brown. Cut into squares.

Nancy Gerhard

ANGEL BISCUITS

5	cups self-rising flour
1	teaspoon soda
3	teaspoons sugar
3/4	cup Crisco
1	yeast cake or 1 package dry yeast in 1/2 cup warm water
2	cups buttermilk

Sift flour, soda and sugar together; cut in shortening and add 1 cup milk and work, then add yeast and more milk. Roll to about 1/4" and cut. Bake at 450°.

Dorothy Edwards

Quotable Kid:

You can't trust your dog to watch your food.
Alex, 4

BEER BREAD

3   cups self-rising flour
3   tablespoons sugar
1   can of beer
    Melted margarine or butter

Mix flour, sugar and beer well. Put ingredients into greased bread pan and bake at 375° for 1 hour. When done, brush melted margarine or butter on top.

Joan Cabai

CLAY'S BEER BATTER BISCUITS

2   cups Bisquick
1   tablespoon sugar
3/4 cup beer*
     Melted butter

Butter muffin tin. Combine all ingredients except butter; mix thoroughly. Fill tins half full. Bake 12 to 14 minutes at 400°. For browner biscuits, brush with butter last 2 minutes of cooking time. Makes 12 delicious muffin-like biscuits.

*Remember, the better the beer, the better the batter!!!

Phil Johnson
Owner, Ile Crocodile

OATMEAL BREAD
(FOUR LOAVES)

10 to 12	cups unbleached flour
2	cups dry oatmeal
2	tablespoons salt
1	cup molasses
1	cup salad oil
2	cups boiling water
2	cups cold water

IN SMALL BOWL:

1/2	cup warm (not hot) water
4	packages active yeast
1	teaspoon sugar

Mix together first 6 ingredients, except for flour, in large bowl and let stand until lukewarm. In a small bowl, combine water, yeast and sugar. When first mixture is lukewarm, add yeast mixture to it. Add 5 to 6 cups unbleached flour and mix well. Add another 5 to 6 cups flour and mix well. Knead in bowl about 5 minutes. Place dough in greased bowl. Cover and let rise 1 1/2 hours. Punch down and rise 45 minutes. Punch down and shape into loaves and place in greased loaf pans. Let rise 30 to 40 minutes. Bake in preheated 400° oven for 25 to 30 minutes. Bread is done when it sounds hollow when you tap the bottom of the loaf. Recipe may be divided in half. Bread may be made into cinnamon oatmeal bread by rolling out loaf before baking, spreading with butter and cinnamon sugar, rolling up and placing in pan to bake.

WHOLE-MEAL IRISH SODA BREAD

1/2	cup sifted white flour
1	teaspoon salt
1	teaspoon baking soda
3/4	cup buttermilk
1 1/2	cups whole wheat flour
1	teaspoon sugar
1/2	teaspoon cream of tartar

Mix dry ingredients with fork. Add buttermilk (if too dry, add more). Knead 10 times. Form circular loaf. Cut deep 1" cross in the top. Bake on cookie sheet at 400° for 50 minutes. Makes 1 loaf.

Mariel Goss
Co-chair, 1st edition
Sanibel-Captiva Cookbook

EASY HEALTH BREAD

1	box All-Bran
1	quart buttermilk
2	tablespoons soda
3 1/2	cups flour, unbleached
4	eggs
1	cup honey
1	teaspoon salt
1 1/2	cups oil
1	cup sugar
1	cup raisins

Place all ingredients in large bowl and mix thoroughly. Pour into 2 large loaf pans or 4 small ones about 2/3 full. Bake for 1 hour at 350°.

NOTE: Floured raisins or boiled raisins distribute better!

Hermine Hartley

SOMETHING LIGHT. . . . JUST RIGHT!

Soups and Salads for Every Appetite

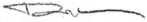

TOO-HOT-FOR-HATTIE
BLACK BEAN GAZPACHO

2	15-ounce cans pinto beans, undrained
1	quart tomato-vegetable juice
2	tablespoons vegetable oil
3	tablespoons lime juice
2	tablespoons Worcestershire sauce
2	teaspoons minced garlic
1	16-ounce jar thick and chunk, medium or hot salsa
1	15-ounce can black beans, rinsed and drained
1	cup chopped, peeled seedless cucumber
1	cup thinly sliced celery
1 1/4	cups cubed, peeled avocado
	Cucumber or celery sticks

Using a food processor or blender, puree pinto beans with their liquid, 2 cups of the tomato-vegetable juice, oil, lime juice, Worcestershire sauce and garlic until smooth. Place mixture into a large bowl and add remaining tomato-vegetable juice, salsa, black beans, chopped cucumber and sliced celery. Chill for a minimum of 3 hours. Add avocado into soup immediately before serving and if desired, garnish with vegetable sticks. Yields 10 to 12 side-dish servings.

Cindy Pierce

AUNTIE KIM'S SUMMER GAZPACHO

1/2	Vidalia, Bermuda or other sweet, white onion, peeled and quartered
1 1/2	firm medium cucumbers, peeled and cut in sections
2	small sweet green peppers, seeded and cut in sections
6	medium to large tomatoes, with stems cut out and quartered
5	large garlic cloves
3/4	cup tomato juice
1/2	cup light olive oil
3/4	teaspoon chili powder
1	small piece of fresh chili pepper
1	tablespoon kosher salt
1/4	cup red wine vinegar
1	tablespoon finely chopped fresh dill
1/4	teaspoon black pepper

In a food processor with the metal chopping blade in place, chop up the onion into fine pieces, turning off and on rapidly for a few seconds. Transfer onion into a bowl. Repeat chopping process with cucumbers, then with the green peppers, adding each to the bowl with the onion. Process 5 of the tomatoes until they are chopped into even small pieces and transfer into bowl with the other chopped ingredients. Process the remaining tomato with the garlic, tomato juice, olive oil, chili powder, chili pepper, kosher salt, red wine vinegar, finely chopped fresh dill and black pepper until a smooth liquid is formed. Mix this liquid with the chopped vegetables and chill in a covered container. Makes 1 1/2 quarts.

NOTE: Vegetables are chopped separately to control the texture of each. You don't have to wash the food processor between vegetables.

Kimberly Smith

HOT OR COLD
TOMATO DILL SOUP

3   pounds chopped fresh tomatoes
3   cups chopped onions
2   quarts chicken stock
1   tablespoon minced orange rind
     Pinch of sugar
1   teaspoon allspice
1   teaspoon garlic powder
     Dill to taste
     Salt and pepper to taste
     Sour cream for garnish

Place all ingredients except sour cream in a large pot and simmer until tomatoes and onions are very tender, about 20 minutes. Allow to cool, then transfer soup to food processor or blender and puree until smooth. Soup may be served hot or cold, garnished with sour cream. Makes 8 to 10 servings.

CREAM OF PEANUT SOUP

1	medium onion, chopped
1/4	cup butter
2	quarts chicken stock
1 3/4	cups light cream
2	stalks celery, chopped
3	tablespoons flour
2	cups smooth peanut butter
	Chopped peanuts

Saute onion and celery in butter until soft, but not brown. Stir in flour until well blended. Add chicken stock, stirring constantly and bring to a boil. Remove from heat and puree in blender. Add peanut butter and cream, stirring to blend thoroughly. Return to low heat, do not boil. Garnish with peanuts.

NOTE: This soup may be served ice cold.

COLD CURRY-SHRIMP SOUP

1 can consommé
1 large package and 1 small package
  cream cheese
2 teaspoons curry
1 medium can small shrimp
2 tablespoons Worcestershire sauce
  Dash of Tabasco sauce
  Dash of cayenne pepper

Wash and dry shrimp and put in blender with 1/3 can of consommé. Mix other ingredients together: cream cheese, curry, Tabasco, cayenne pepper and Worcestershire sauce. Pour these in blender, thoroughly blend and pour into custard cups; refrigerate until stiff. Remove from refrigerator. Add a little of remaining liquid consommé to each cup and refrigerate again until top is set. Makes 6 servings.

Ted McRae

Quotable Kid:

When you're dressed up like a princess,
it's easier to act like one.
Kelly, 6

CHILLED LIME AND HONEYDEW SOUP

1	very ripe honeydew melon
1/4	cup chicken stock
1/4	cup lime juice
1/4	cup sour cream
1 1/2	tablespoons chutney
	Nutmeg

Place ingredients in blender or food processor and puree until smooth. Chill, garnish with nutmeg.

Karen Valentine

CHILLED AVOCADO SOUP

2   ripe avocados, peeled and seeded
4   cups chicken broth
2   cups light cream
1   teaspoon curry powder
4   tablespoons light rum
1   teaspoon salt
     Ground pepper
     Juice of 1/2 to 1 lemon
2   lemons, sliced for garnish

Blend all ingredients, except sliced lemons, until smooth. May have to be done in batches and then blended all together in bowl. Chill at least 4 hours and serve with lemon garnish in chilled bowls. Makes 6 servings.

Milena Eskew

CHILLED CUCUMBER AND SPINACH SOUP

2	tablespoons butter
1	large onion, chopped
1	pound fresh spinach
4	cups chicken broth (MBT instant)
1 to 1 1/2	pounds cucumber, peeled, seeded and chopped
8	ounces cream cheese
2	tablespoons lemon juice
1/2	cup half and half

Melt butter in large pot and saute onion until tender. Wash and stem the spinach, add it to the onion in pot and stir until the spinach is wilted. Add the chicken broth and cucumber, simmer for 20 minutes. Process in blender in batches. Return to pot and add the cream cheese (cut in pieces). Stir over low heat, until the cheese is melted. Add lemon juice, salt and pepper. Remove from heat, add half and half. Chill well. Serves 6.

NOTE: For a different soup, delete the spinach and add several sizable sprigs of fresh dill to the blender before processing.

Mariel Goss
Co-chair, 1st edition
Sanibel-Captiva Cookbook

CITRUS-BEET SOUP

1	tablespoon canola oil
1	cup chopped onion
2	large cloves garlic, crushed
1 1/2	tablespoons sugar
1	Valencia orange
2	pounds beets (without tops), peeled and cut in 1" pieces
2	14-ounce cans beef broth plus 1 can water
1	cup each peeled and diced potato and canned tomatoes, seeded
2 1/2	tablespoons balsamic vinegar
1	teaspoon salt
	Reduced-fat sour cream, snipped fresh dill, lemon slices and freshly ground pepper as garnish

Heat oil on medium-low heat in a large stock pot. Stir in onion, garlic and sugar; cook until onion is translucent. Prepare orange zest by stripping 3 to 4" long sections of peel with a vegetable peeler or knife. Press or squeeze the orange and set juice aside. Add zest, along with the beets, broth, water, potatoes, tomatoes, vinegar and salt, to the stock pot. Bring to a boil, reduce heat, cover and simmer until beets are tender (about 45 minutes). Remove from heat and let soup cool for 15 minutes. Remove orange zest. Puree the beet soup in a food processor or blender in several batches, adding the reserved orange juice to the puree. Place in a large bowl and chill for several hours or up to 3 days prior to serving. If desired, garnish each serving with a dollop of sour cream, dill, lemon slice and ground pepper.

Cindy Pierce

COLD CUCUMBER SOUP

2	cups peeled, seeded cucumbers, cut in pieces
1 1/2	cups chicken stock
1	cup diced celery, including some leaves
1	green onion, diced
1/4	cup parsley
1/4	cup fresh dill
2	tablespoons flour
2	tablespoons butter
	Salt and pepper
1	cup light cream
	Fresh dill, chopped fine for garnish

Place first 6 ingredients in a blender and blend thoroughly; set aside. In an enamel saucepan, make a roux of the butter and flour, stirring well. Add the contents of the blender and bring to a boil, stirring. Reduce heat to a simmer and cook for 5 minutes and stir. Add the salt and pepper to taste. Chill in the refrigerator and before serving, whisk in the cream. Pour in the soup cups and garnish with fresh dill. This can be made one day ahead.

Kimberly Smith

AVOCADO, BACON, CHIVE-CHEESE AND TOMATO SANDWICH

1	pound bacon, cooked crisp and chopped
2	medium ripe tomatoes, sliced thin
1	8-ounce package cream cheese, room temperature
1/4	cup fresh chives, chopped
2	teaspoons lemon juice
4	drops hot sauce
2	ripe avocados, sliced
1/4	teaspoon salt
	Fresh ground pepper
	Lettuce leaves
1	loaf Italian bread

Chop bacon; set aside. Slice tomatoes; set aside. Combine cream cheese, chives, lemon juice and hot pepper sauce. Beat until smooth.

TO ASSEMBLE: Split bread lengthwise, but do not cut through. Open carefully and hollow out loaf, leaving 1/2" shell in each half. Spread cheese mixture over bottom half and sprinkle with bacon, patting gently into place. Peel and slice avocado. Toss with remaining lemon juice and arrange over bacon. Top with tomato slices. Sprinkle with salt and pepper. Arrange single layer of lettuce leaves over tomatoes. Close sandwich and press together gently. To serve, cut diagonally into wedges. A great summer sandwich!

Sharon Chamberlain

RED AND YELLOW TOMATO SOUP

1	tablespoon extra-virgin olive oil
1	yellow bell pepper, cut in 1" pieces
3	large shallots, sliced
2	large cloves garlic, sliced
4	pounds yellow tomatoes, cut in 1" chunks
2	sprigs fresh oregano
2	14-ounce cans vegetable broth and 1/2 cup water
1 1/2	teaspoons salt
	Diced red tomato, julienned basil, freshly ground pepper as garnish

Heat oil over medium-high heat in a large soup pot. Add bell pepper, shallots and garlic; cook for 5 minutes. Add tomatoes and oregano; continue cooking for 5 minutes. Add broth, water and salt. Partially cover the pot and simmer for 20 minutes. Remove the oregano and cool the soup for 30 minutes. Remove the skins and seeds from the tomato mixture by passing it through a fine sieve, in batches. Transfer to a large bowl and chill for several hours or up to 3 days prior to serving. If desired, garnish each serving with diced red tomato, basil and ground pepper.

Cindy Pierce

JOSHUA'S SANIBEL BOUILLABAISSE

3	boxes Knorr bouillabaisse seafood mix
5	tablespoons vegetable or olive oil
7	cups water
1	can peeled tomatoes in water, diced
1 1/2	cups white wine
	Fresh pressed garlic to taste
	Green onion (or any onion), diced, to taste
1/2	teaspoon sugar
2 to 4	potatoes, peeled and diced
2	cubes Knorr fish bouillon (if available)
	Salt to taste
1	pound bay scallops
2 to 3	pounds fish, use a combination of 2 to 3 of the following: grouper, snapper, swordfish, tuna, mahi-mahi, flounder, or cod/scrod (do not use shark or salmon)
1	pound frozen popcorn shrimp (optional)
1 to 2	dozen mussels or clams (optional)

In a large pot, combine bouillabaisse mix, oil and water; bring to a boil. Add tomatoes, wine, garlic, onion, sugar, potatoes, bouillon and salt. Return to a boil. Reduce heat and simmer until potatoes are almost done. Add scallops, fish and mussels or clams (if desired) and return to a boil. Reduce heat and simmer 5 minutes or until fish is done. Add popcorn shrimp (if desired) and simmer until shrimp are warm. Serve.

Jerry Sheets

ZUPPA DI PESCE

	*Fish stock or 1 bottle clam juice
1/2	clove garlic
3	fillets anchovy
1	dry red pepper
1/2	glass dry white wine
1/2	glass oil
1	tablespoon tomato paste or 4 to 5 fresh tomatoes, peeled

Crush together the garlic, anchovy and pepper. Pour the wine over it and mix. In a deep pan, heat the oil and add the wine mixture and tomatoes. Add crab and strip of cod and simmer. Add stock, more fish and hot water. Season and cook 15 minutes. Serve with slices of toast and garnish with parsley.

*Fish: shrimp, cod, crab, lobster, clams, scallops, haddock, flounder.

Sylvia Mintz

SNOOK CHOWDER

1	cup celery and onions, chopped
3	tablespoons flour
	Assorted vegetables
	Butter
3	cups milk
	Cooked and flaked snook

Brown approximately 1 cup of celery and onions in butter until soft. Blend 3 tablespoons flour, stir constantly until heated. Stir in approximately 3 cups milk, cooking until it thickens. Bring to boil, reduce heat and add assorted vegetables (e.g. carrots, peas, corn, green beans, potatoes, etc., diced to a small size). Bring again to a boil, reduce heat and cook slowly until vegetables are tender. Stir in cooked, flaked snook and cook until heated.

NOTE: This is a great "leftovers" dish, for the snook and vegetables. Goes great with corn bread or some other good breads.

Betty Anholt

MARY'S FISH SOUP

3	tablespoons butter
2	medium onions, chopped
1/2	green pepper, chopped
1/2	cup celery, chopped
1	clove garlic, minced
1 1/2	tablespoons flour
1	20- ounce can stewed tomatoes
1/2	large can Clamato or "V-8" juice
1	tablespoon salt (optional)
1	bottle clam juice
2	tablespoons sugar
4	bay leaves
1	tablespoon dried thyme
1/2	teaspoon allspice
3	tablespoons Worcestershire sauce
1/4	tablespoon hot pepper sauce (Tabasco)
1	7-ounce can tuna, drained
1	7-ounce can shrimp, undrained
1	can clams, undrained
1	large fresh or frozen fish (any kind)

Melt butter, add onions, pepper, celery and garlic. Cook until tender. Blend in flour. Add tomatoes, Clamato or "V-8" juice, salt, sugar, bay leaves, thyme, allspice, Worcestershire sauce and hot pepper sauce. Simmer 15 minutes. Add tuna, shrimp, clams, clam juice and fish. Simmer 15 minutes more. Serve with warm brandy.

Mary Tenbroek

PEARL'S GUMBO

	Boiling chicken or shrimp
1/4	pound salt pork or smoked bacon, diced
2	cups green peppers, diced
2	cups onions
2	cloves garlic
1	tablespoon flour
3 or 4	fresh tomatoes or 1 small can tomatoes
1	pound cut up okra
2	leaves sweet basil or some dry basil
2	teaspoons chopped parsley
1/2	cup chopped celery (optional)
	Lawry's salt and pepper to taste

Boil a chicken (or shrimp). Bone the chicken, save the stock. Fry 1/4 pound salt pork (or smoked bacon). Use all bacon, diced and 4 tablespoons of drippings. Brown flour in bacon drippings. Add all the vegetables and mix thoroughly. Either fry garlic cloves in drippings or mince and use with other vegetables. Add chicken stock until it is a rich gravy. Add chicken and cook until the vegetables are cooked. Add more stock or water, if needed. If you use boiled shrimp, add them about 2 minutes before you take the gumbo off the stove. You may use filé powder, but it is not necessary. Lawry's salt and pepper to taste.

NOTE: If you want jambalaya, add cooked chicken, shrimp, ham, lobster, pork, "craw-dads" or other meat or seafood (except fish) just before you take it off the stove. A few drops of Tabasco sauce is good, but optional.

Pearl Stokes

COQUINA BROTH

	Fresh coquinas
1	small carrot, grated finely
1	small stalk celery, grated finely
	Water
	Pinch of salt
	White pepper (optional)
2	potatoes, chopped finely (optional)

Fill large kettle half full of clean, fresh coquinas, completely cover with cold water. Bring to a boil. (Coquinas will open up and fill kettle.) Boil for 3 to 5 minutes. Drain broth into smaller pan. If potatoes are used, add to broth. Return to heat (medium). Add grated carrot and celery. Season to taste and serve. Coquinas have a very delicate flavor and are best as a fairly clear broth.

NOTE: To gather coquinas, make a square or rectangular shadow box, cover bottom with 1/4" screening to allow sand and debris to sift through.

Mary Aleck

ISLAND CLAM CHOWDER

24	clams
1/4	pound salt pork
4	onions, diced
6	carrots, diced
4	cups cubed potatoes
2	stalks celery
1	can tomatoes
1	tablespoon salt
5	quarts water
1/2	cup flour
1/4	teaspoon pepper
1/4	teaspoon thyme

Open clams and chop, reserving liquid. Bring liquid to a boil and strain. Add sliced onions, fried with salt, pork, diced vegetables, tomatoes, water and salt. Then cook for 3 hours. Add pepper, thyme and thicken with flour moistened with water. Makes 8 to 10 servings.

NOTE: This is a very hearty soup and wonderful to take in a thermos on a boat on a cool day. Also makes a good Sunday night supper dish served with warm bread or rolls and desserts. May be frozen.

John Veenschoten

Kitchen Tid-Bit:

Before opening clams, arrange them in a single layer in a pan and place in the freezer for about 15 minutes. The intense cold relaxes the clams' muscles and makes opening them a snap.

EUGENIE'S MANHATTAN CLAM CHOWDER

1/2	pound bacon, diced and fried
1	large onion, chopped
6	small carrots, thin sliced
3	stalks celery
1	tablespoon parsley flakes
1	28-ounce can tomatoes
	Salt and pepper to taste
1	pound whole fresh baby clams or 2 to 3 cans clams with liquid
1	8-ounce bottle clam juice
1	cup tomato juice
1	bay leaf
1/4	teaspoon powdered thyme
6	medium potatoes, pared and sliced

Layer all ingredients in a large pot. Simmer until vegetables are tender, about 1 hour.

Eugenia Kontinos Loughney
Co-chair, 1st edition
Sanibel-Captiva Cookbook

NEW ENGLAND CLAM CHOWDER

2	dozen cherrystone clams, well scrubbed (may substitute 2 cans chopped clams)
2	cups water
4	ounces slab bacon, cut into 1/2" dice
2	tablespoons unsalted butter
1	large onion, peeled and cut into 1/4" dice
1/4	cup unbleached all-purpose flour
6	potatoes, peeled and cut into 1/2" dice (about 4 cups)
2	teaspoons dried thyme
	Freshly ground black pepper to taste
2	cups milk
2	cups heavy or whipping cream
3	tablespoons chopped fresh Italian parsley

Add clams to 2 cups of water in a large soup pot. Cover and cook over medium heat until clams open. Remove from heat and cool for 10 minutes. Discard any clams whose shells don't open. Remove the meat from the clam shells, coarsely chop; set aside. Strain broth; set aside.

Brown the bacon over low heat in the soup pot. Add butter and onions. Cook for 10 minutes or until onions are translucent. Add flour and continue to cook, stirring, for another 5 minutes. Add clam broth, potatoes, thyme and pepper; simmer for 5 minutes. Add chopped clams and simmer for 12 to 15 minutes or until clams are tender. Add milk and cream; stir over low heat until soup is hot. Be careful not to boil the milk or it will curdle. Stir in parsley, adjust seasonings and serve hot. Yields 10 to 12 servings.

Liz Fowler

CLEMENTINE'S CLAM CHOWDER

8 to 10   potatoes, diced
6 to 8   onions, diced
1/2   pound white bacon (salt pork)
1   quart chopped clams
1   medium can tomatoes or 1 cup
      tomato puree
      Boiling water
      Salt and pepper to taste

Dice potatoes, onions and salt pork (white bacon). Fry the salt pork until light brown in large pot. Add 1 quart of chopped clams to bacon and drippings. Stir and cook for about 10 minutes. Add diced potatoes and onions; mix thoroughly. Add some black pepper and tomatoes or tomato puree. Add boiling water to not quite cover. Bring to boil and cook until juice is a rich gravy (about 1 hour). Add more hot water if necessary. Do not boil hard, but more than a simmer. Do not add salt until nearly done, then add only if needed.

NOTE: If using canned clams, do not add until just before you add the tomatoes.

My grandparents came to Sanibel in 1900. There were clams in the Bay, tomatoes in the fields and they had white bacon, potatoes and onions. My grandmother, Clementine Gibson, invented her own clam chowder. It was so good, she never changed it. She found the blending very important.

Pearl Stokes

AVGOLEMONO
(GREEK CHICKEN SOUP)

6   cups chicken broth
1   cup uncooked rice
4   eggs, separated
     Juice of 2 lemons
     Salt and pepper to taste

Bring broth to boil. Add rice and cook until tender. In large mixing bowl, beat the egg whites until stiff. Slowly add the yolks and lemon juice until well blended. Then add the broth, a little at a time, beating well until most of the broth is used. Pour this mixture back into the pot, stirring well. Pieces of chicken may be added. Serve soup immediately.

NOTE: This traditional chicken soup is the pride of Greek cuisine.

Eugenia Kontinos Loughney
Co-chair, 1st edition
Sanibel-Captiva Cookbook

GREEK LEMON SOUP

4   cups strained chicken broth
1/4 cup uncooked rice
3   eggs
     Juice of 1 lemon
     Salt
     White pepper

Heat chicken broth in a saucepan. Add rice. Cover and simmer for about 25 minutes or until rice is tender. Beat eggs and lemon juice. Add 1/2 cup chicken broth to the egg mixture, one tablespoon at a time, stirring constantly. Stir mixture into remaining hot soup. Serve hot.

BLEU CHEESE SOUP WITH BACON

2	chopped onions
3	chopped celery sticks
3	chopped carrots
1	chopped potato
6	tablespoons butter
1	cup white wine
3	cups chicken stock
1/2 to 3/4	pound bleu cheese
	Salt and pepper to taste
	Bacon bits for garnish

Saute onions, celery, carrots and potato in butter for a few minutes. Add wine and chicken stock; simmer until vegetables are very tender, about 20 to 30 minutes. Set aside to cool. Place soup in food processor or blender and puree, adding 1/2 to 3/4 pound bleu cheese and salt and pepper to taste. To serve, slowly reheat the soup and garnish with crisp bacon bits.

Karen Valentine

ANITA'S MINESTRONE

1/4	cup salad oil
1	clove garlic, finely chopped
1/2	cup chopped onion
2	stalks celery with leaves, chopped
2	medium carrots, pared and diced
1	can tomatoes, undrained
3	beef bouillon cubes
2	cups pared, diced potatoes
1	cup chopped cabbage
3	tablespoons chopped parsley
2	teaspoons salt
1/4	teaspoon black pepper
1	teaspoon dried marjoram
1/4	teaspoon dried rosemary
1	cup uncooked ditalini
1	10-ounce package frozen peas
1	can red kidney beans
	Grated Parmesan cheese

Heat oil in 6-quart kettle. Add garlic, onion and celery; saute until tender, about 5 minutes. Add carrots, tomatoes, bouillon cubes, potatoes, cabbage, parsley, salt, pepper, herbs and 6 cups water or more. Bring to boil, reduce hat and simmer, covered, 40 minutes. Add ditalini, peas and kidney beans. Bring back to boiling. Reduce heat and simmer 20 minutes longer. Serve with cheese sprinkled on top.

Marjorie Wilson

CARROT-COCONUT BISQUE

	Cooking spray
1	cup washed, sliced leeks (white part only)
1	tablespoon minced, peeled gingerroot
1 1/2	teaspoons salt
1/2	teaspoon ground coriander
4	cups thinly sliced, peeled carrots (1 1/2 pounds)
1/4	cup basmati rice
3	cups each vegetable broth and water
1	12-ounce can evaporated skim milk
1	teaspoon coconut extract
1/4	teaspoon ground white pepper
	Nonfat plain yogurt and carrot curls as garnish

Spray bottom of large stock pot with cooking spray. Add leeks, gingerroot, salt and coriander. Cook, covered, over medium-low heat for 15 minutes. Stir occasionally using a wooden spoon. Add carrots, rice, broth, water, skim milk, coconut extract and pepper to the pot; bring to a boil. Lower the heat, cover and simmer 25 minutes or until carrots and rice are fully cooked. Remove pot from heat and cool the soup for 15 minutes. Puree the soup in a food processor or blender in several batches. Place in a large bowl and chill, covered, for several hours or up to 3 days prior to serving. If desired, garnish each serving with a dollop of yogurt and carrot curls.

BRAZILIAN CHICKEN RICE SOUP
(CHALMERS ALWAYS ASKS FOR MORE!)

1	3-pound chicken
1	bay leaf
1	medium sized onion, quartered
1	whole clove
2	ripe tomatoes, quartered
1	carrot, cut into 1" pieces
1/4	cup chopped celery leaves
20	black peppercorns, tied in a piece of cheesecloth
1/2	cup uncooked white rice
	Salt and freshly ground black pepper
3	carrots, thinly sliced on the diagonal
3	stalks celery, thinly sliced on the diagonal
1/4	cup finely chopped flat-leaf parsley

Remove fat and skin from the chicken. Put the chicken in a large soup pot with tomatoes, onion quarters, carrot pieces, celery leaves and peppercorn bundle. On one of the onion quarters, pin the bay leaf along with the clove. Add 10 cups cold water and bring to a boil. Reduce heat and simmer for 1 hour, skimming off fat and foam periodically from the surface. Remove chicken and let it cool. Strain the broth through a sieve, pressing vegetables to remove the juices. When chicken is cool, remove meat from the bones and shred or finely dice it. Add rice, salt and pepper to the broth and cook over low heat for 10 minutes. Add thinly sliced carrots and celery, chicken and half of the parsley. Simmer for 10 minutes or until rice is cooked. Add salt and pepper to taste; sprinkle with remaining parsley. Serve hot. Yields 8 as an appetizer, 4 to 6 as an entreé.

NOTE: This recipe includes instructions for making the broth. If in a hurry, use a good canned stock and start recipe with adding the rice.

Kevin Pierce

TRY THIS THAI SOUP!

2	tablespoons sweet butter
1/4	cup chopped onion
2	tablespoons chopped lemon grass
2	tablespoons chopped fresh ginger
1/2	teaspoon red pepper flakes
1	chili pepper, seeded, deribbed and chopped
4	cups vegetable broth
2	whole chicken breasts, skinned and boned
2	tablespoons sliced scallions
2	tablespoons peeled, seeded and diced tomato
2	tablespoons chopped cilantro
1	cup coconut milk
1	cup button mushrooms, cut into large dice
2	tablespoons fish sauce (nam pla)
	Salt to taste

In a large saute pan, heat butter over medium-high heat until it is melted. Add onion, lemon grass, ginger, red pepper flakes and chili pepper; cook until onion is tender. Add broth and cook for 10 minutes. Add chicken breasts, cover and cook for 5 minutes. Remove the chicken, chop it into a large dice and place it in a soup tureen. Add scallions, tomato and cilantro to the tureen as well. Strain broth through a sieve, discarding solids. Add coconut milk and mushrooms to the strained broth and bring to a boil. Add the fish sauce and continue cooking for 5 minutes. Season with salt to taste and add the broth to the tureen.

NOTE: Add rice to this and it becomes a complete meal!

Kevin Pierce

BAKED POTATO SOUP

1/2	stick butter
1	small onion, chopped
2	tablespoons all-purpose flour
6 to 8	cups milk
6	baked potatoes with skin, cubed
4	slices cooked bacon, crumbled
1/2	cup shredded sharp Cheddar cheese
1	8-ounce container sour cream

TOPPINGS:

2	slices cooked bacon, crumbled
1/3	cup shredded sharp Cheddar cheese
1/4	cup chopped green onions

Melt butter in large stock pot. Add onion and cook until tender. Add flour and mix thoroughly. Add milk and potatoes, then mix and heat thoroughly. Add 4 slices crumbled bacon, 1/2 cup cheese and sour cream. Top individual servings with sprinklings of bacon, cheese and green onions.

Cindy Sitton

SPRING FRUIT SALAD
WITH POPPY SEED DRESSING

FRUIT SALAD:

1/2	small pineapple or 4-ounce can pineapple chunks
1	large orange or 11-ounce can mandarin oranges
1	pint strawberries, cut in halves
1/4	cucumber, sliced (prefer gourmet type)
6	lettuce cups

POPPY SEED DRESSING:

3/4	cup sugar
1/3	cup cider vinegar
1	teaspoon dry mustard
1	teaspoon salt
1 1/2	teaspoons onion juice
1	cup vegetable oil
1 1/2	tablespoons poppy seed

Divide and arrange fruits and cucumber slices between lettuce cups. Blend first 5 dressing ingredients together in food processor or blender. Add the vegetable oil slowly while blending. Add poppy seed and stir to blend. Pour dressing over salad just before serving.

Marjorie Anderson

GRAPEFRUIT SALAD
WITH POPPY SEED DRESSING

2	heads romaine lettuce, washed and dried
4	white grapefruits, sectioned
1	Bermuda onion, thinly sliced

DRESSING:

1	cup apple juice
6	tablespoons fresh lemon juice
4	tablespoons Dijon mustard
2	tablespoons honey
1	tablespoon poppy seeds
1	teaspoon black pepper

Break lettuce into small pieces and peel membrane from grapefruit sections. Arrange lettuce on salad plates and top with grapefruit sections (approximately 1/2 of a grapefruit per plate) and onion slices.

DRESSING: Mix together ingredients until smooth. Dress each salad with approximately 2 tablespoons.

Cindy Pierce

Kitchen Tid-Bit:

Individual peeled segments of lemon, lime, orange and grapefruit are a wonderful garnish (not to mention a great snack!). The secret to preparing whole, membrane- and pith-free segments lies in the approach: First cut off both ends of the fruit with a sharp paring knife and set the fruit flat on a work surface. Work the knife down along the natural rounded shape of the fruit, cutting off both the bitter pith and peel. Then hold the peeled fruit and slice down between the membranes to free each segment.

LEXINGTON BARBECUE SLAW

1	head cabbage, grated fine
1/4	cup sugar
1/4	cup cider vinegar
3/4	cup ketchup
1/4	cup barbecue sauce
1/8	teaspoon cayenne pepper
1/4	teaspoon Tabasco sauce
	Salt and pepper to taste

Combine sugar and vinegar; stir until sugar is dissolved. Add next 5 ingredients and stir into grated cabbage. Refrigerate overnight. Excellent with smoked pork barbecue.

Cindy Sitton

DELICIOUS COLESLAW

1	cup salad oil
1	cup vinegar
1/4	cup white sugar
2	medium cabbages, shredded
1	onion, diced
2	carrots, grated
2	teaspoons celery seed

Heat oil, vinegar and sugar. Pour over vegetables. Add celery seeds; mix well. This coleslaw will keep up to 2 1/2 weeks in refrigerator.

Jennie Steenuis

CANADIAN CITRUS SALAD

3	tablespoons red wine vinegar
2	tablespoons fruit nectar (e.g. guava or mango)
1	tablespoon minced shallot
1	teaspoon minced garlic
	Salt and pepper to taste
1/2	cup olive oil
8	cups assorted salad greens
1	large orange and 1 blood orange, peeled, pith removed, sliced in rounds
1	small red onion, sliced into rings
1/4	cup pimento-stuffed green olives
1/4	cup pitted kalamata olives

Prepare dressing by mixing together vinegar, fruit nectar, shallot, garlic, salt and pepper; then blending in oil. Lightly dress salad greens. In a medium bowl, add oranges, half of the onion rings, olives and remaining dressing. Place greens on serving platter and top with orange slices, onion and olives.

Kas Chenciner

SUNSHINE CITRUS SPINACH SALAD

1/4	cup fresh Florida grapefruit juice
2	tablespoons honey
2	tablespoons olive oil
1 1/2	tablespoons Worcestershire sauce
1	teaspoon crushed dried oregano
2	garlic cloves, minced
1/4	teaspoon each salt and freshly cracked black pepper
6	cups or 1/2 pound fresh spinach leaves, stems removed
2	large Florida red grapefruit, peeled and sectioned
1	small avocado, peeled and cut into bite size pieces
1/2	cup toasted chopped walnuts
1/2	cup crumbled goat cheese

Prepare dressing by mixing together the first 7 ingredients in a small bowl. In serving bowl, add spinach, grapefruit, avocado and walnuts. Toss with dressing and top with crumbled goat cheese.

Cindy Pierce

SWEET AND SOUR CUCUMBERS

2	medium size cucumbers
3	scallions
6	radishes
1	sprig parsley, snipped
1	tablespoon tarragon vinegar
1	tablespoon sugar
1	tablespoon vegetable oil
	Salt and pepper to taste
1	tablespoon fresh crushed herbs, if available

Peel and slice the cucumbers as thinly as possible. Slice scallions very thin, including the tops. Then add sliced radishes and snipped parsley. Combine vinegar, sugar and oil; pour over cucumber mixture. Toss, season to taste and refrigerate 1 hour before serving. Makes about 2 cups.

Joan Cabai

CUCUMBER AND ONION SALAD

3	tablespoons sugar
2	tablespoons oil (olive or vegetable)
1/3	cup cider vinegar
1	cup water
	Freshly ground pepper to taste
1/2	teaspoon salt
4	cucumbers
1	red onion, sliced

Prepare dressing by mixing together sugar, oil, vinegar, water, salt and pepper. Slice cucumbers and onions; mix together. Add dressing and chill. Best when prepared 12 to 24 hours in advance.

Lee Harder

HEART OF PALM SALAD

	Romaine lettuce
	Iceberg lettuce
1/2	cup salami, cut in narrow strips
2 or 3	hearts of palm, coarsely chopped
1/2	of a sweet red or green pepper
3	tablespoons olive oil
1	tablespoon vinegar
1/2	of a lemon
1	teaspoon Worcestershire sauce
	Pinch of dry mustard
	Salt to taste
	Pepper to taste
1	tablespoon grated Parmesan cheese

SALAD: Rub salad bowl thoroughly with garlic, add equal parts romaine and iceberg lettuce. Toss in salami, hearts of palm, and sweet red or green pepper.

DRESSING: Combine oil, vinegar, lemon juice, Worcestershire sauce, mustard, salt and pepper. Sprinkle with grated Parmesan cheese and toss well.

Rosalie Isom

EASY CAESAR VIA MONTREAL

3	tablespoons white wine vinegar
1	teaspoon salt
1	teaspoon dry mustard
1	clove garlic, crushed
1/2	teaspoon pepper
1	egg
1/2	cup grated Parmesan cheese
1	cup olive oil
	Romaine lettuce
	Croutons

Mix first 7 ingredients in blender for a few seconds. Then add oil gradually. Blend until smooth. Toss desired amount of dressing with bite-size pieces of romaine lettuce and croutons and serve.

Kas Chenciner

SAM'S FLORIDA TOSSED SALAD

1	head romaine lettuce, torn into pieces
1	head leaf lettuce, torn into pieces
1	11-ounce can mandarin oranges
1/3	cup slivered almonds
1	cup fresh mushrooms, sliced
1	large avocado, diced
4	green onions
3/4	cup Romano cheese, grated

DRESSING:

1/4	cup vegetable oil
2	tablespoons sugar
2	tablespoons vinegar
1/2	teaspoon salt

Toss all salad ingredients. Mix dressing ingredients; pour over salad.

Liz Fowler

"HELEN'S HORRENDOUS" ASPIC SALAD

1	package strawberry gelatin
1	heaping teaspoon cream-style prepared horseradish
2	cups tomato juice

Make strawberry gelatin according to directions on package except use tomato juice in place of water and add horseradish. Pour into pint mold (or use 4 to 6 individual molds if desired) and chill until firm.

NOTE: This is really Helen Morgenroth's (Captiva) recipe. When she gave it to me I said, "Helen you're kidding, it sounds horrendous!" Hence the name, a misnomer as it really is delicious. Try it. You'll agree.

SERVING SUGGESTIONS: This aspic can be served by itself on a lettuce leaf, plain or with mayonnaise. It is great with shrimp or flaked fish salad. If you use a ring mold, it makes a very colorful dish when arranged on a bed of crisp green lettuce leaves, filled with shrimp or fish salad and served with mayonnaise.

Pintard Mills

GREEN BEAN SALAD

1	can green beans, drained, or equivalent in fresh, lightly steamed
1/3	cup Miracle French dressing
1/2	cup sour cream
1	teaspoon horseradish
1/2	teaspoon seasoned salt
1/2	teaspoon dry mustard
1	toaspoon Italian ocasoning

Mix together while warm and let stand in refrigerator overnight.

Pearl Smith

ORANGE-CAULIFLOWER SALAD

2	10-ounce cans mandarin oranges
4	cups uncooked cauliflowerets
3/4	cup chopped green peppers
6	cups bite size pieces spinach

DRESSING:

1/2	cup oil
1/2	cup vinegar
1/4	teaspoon salt
1/4	teaspoon black pepper
1	teaspoon mustard
3	teaspoons sugar
1	crushed clove garlic
2	tablespoons heavy cream

Combine oranges, cauliflowerets, green pepper and spinach in a large salad bowl. Mix dressing ingredients together: oil, vinegar, salt, mustard, sugar, black pepper, garlic and cream. Place in bottle and shake well. Serves 14.

Lois Cassavell

BROCCOLI SALAD

1	bunch fresh broccoli
2	large stalks celery, chopped fine
1/4	cup green olives, sliced thin
3/4	cup mayonnaise
1	bunch green onions, whites only
3	hard-boiled eggs, chopped
1	tablespoon lemon juice

Boil broccoli 3 minutes (use only small stems and buds); drain well. Cut broccoli in small pieces. If using a food processor, chop a couple of seconds. In dish, layer broccoli, onions (white part only), celery, eggs and olives. Mix together lemon juice and mayonnaise. Pour this mixture over broccoli, onions, celery, eggs and olives. Blend just enough for mayonnaise to mix with ingredients. Chill 3 hours or overnight.

Mrs. Edward Hayes

Kitchen Tid-Bit:

For perfect hard-boiled eggs, start with eggs that are room temperatrue. In a pot large enough to boil the eggs in a single layer, bring cold water to a boil. When the water is boiling, not before, place the eggs in the pot. Boil 8 minutes for small eggs, 10 for large ones. Remove the eggs and cool immediately in several changes of cold water.

ST. MAARTEN SALAD
(EXCELLENT WITH FISH!)

1	3-ounce package lime gelatin
1	cup boiling water
2	cups grated cucumber
1	teaspoon grated onion
1	3-ounce package softened cream cheese
1/2	cup mayonnaise
	Salt to taste
1	teaspoon lemon or lime juice
1	teaspoon vinegar

Dissolve gelatin in boiling water; chill thoroughly. Combine cucumber, onion and cream cheese. Stir in mayonnaise, salt, lemon juice and vinegar; mix well. Stir into chilled gelatin mixture; chill until firm.

Rosalie Isom

SHRIMP AND COLESLAW ASPIC

3	envelopes gelatin
3	cups water
2 1/4	cups mayonnaise
9	tablespoons lemon juice
3	tablespoons grated onion
9	drops liquid pepper seasoning
3 3/4	teaspoon salt
2 1/4	cups finely chopped cabbage
2 1/4	cups finely grated carrot
4	cups cooked shrimp

Heat gelatin and 1 cup water until dissolved. Add rest of water and mayonnaise, lemon juice, onion, pepper and salt; mix well, cool. Add cabbage, carrot and 3 cups of the shrimp; chill until thick. Mix well and spoon into 9-cup mold; chill until firm. Turn out onto serving dish and decorate with remaining cup of shrimp and greens. Serves 12.

Lois Van Arsdell

CARROT VINAIGRETTE

8	carrots, pared and cut in julienne strips
2	tablespoons vinegar
1	teaspoon salt
1	teaspoon sugar
1/2	teaspoon fresh lemon juice
1/4	cup water
2	tablespoons salad oil
1/8	teaspoon pepper, fresh ground
1/4	teaspoon dried dill
2	tablespoons chopped fresh green onions

Place carrots and water in flat saucepan. Cover and cook over low heat for 15 to 20 minutes until carrots are crisp tender. Remove from heat and drain. Combine other ingredients in large bowl, add carrots and mix well. Cover and chill for several hours.

Jean Cate

SHELLS WITH UNCOOKED TOMATO, BASIL AND MOZZARELLA SAUCE

1 1/2	pounds plum or cherry tomatoes
1/2	cup extra-virgin olive oil
1/4	cup fresh basil leaves, torn into small pieces or chopped or 1/4 cup chopped fresh Italian parsley
1/2	pound fresh mozzarella, cut into small dice (must be fresh!)
1 to 2	cloves garlic, finely chopped
2	tablespoons small capers, drained
1/4	teaspoon red pepper flakes (or to taste)
1	teaspoon salt
1	pound pasta shells

Seed tomatoes and remove tough area around core. Slice into quarters lengthwise and then coarsely chop. Quarter the cherry tomatoes if using them. Stir in olive oil, basil or parsley, mozzarella, garlic, capers, red pepper flakes and salt with the tomatoes. Sauce should then be covered and left at room temperature while pasta cooks or up to 4 hours in advance. Prepare pasta shells according to package directions. Add pasta to sauce and serve.

Cindy Pierce

Kitchen Tid-Bit:

Cut fresh herbs easily by removing leaves from the stems and stacking them. Roll the leaves lengthwise tightly. With a small knife, cut thin strips across the rolled budle of leaves. This creates long, thin julienned slices of herb. For finely minced herbs, turn the julienned slices (still rolled) and cut crosswise into very thin strips.

GREEK RAVIOLI PASTA SALAD

2	9-ounce boxes cheese ravioli, cooked
2	bunches asparagus, cooked
1	cup green onion, chopped
1	yellow squash, finely chopped
1	zucchini, chopped
8	ounces feta cheese
4	ounces semi-hard cheese, such as Swiss, grated
1	6-ounce can pitted black olives
1	tomato, diced

LEMON DRESSING:

1/2	cup olive oil
1/4	cup lemon juice
2	tablespoons tarragon vinegar
3	tablespoons sugar
2	tablespoons minced green onion
1	teaspoon salt
1/2	teaspoon dry mustard
	Dash of black pepper

Mix lemon dressing ingredients in a glass jar. Pour over salad ingredients and toss. Serve well chilled.

Sharon Chamberlain

TANGY BEET AND POTATO SALAD

1 1/2	pounds small red potatoes
2	bunches fresh beets, washed and with all but 1" of stems removed
1	bunch scallions, thinly sliced
2	tablespoons grainy prepared mustard
1	teaspoon horseradish
1	tablespoon olive oil
1 1/2	tablespoons red wine vinegar
	Salt and pepper to taste

Place potatoes in pan with enough water to cover them halfway and boil for 15 minutes. Add beets and continue to boil until beets are tender, approximately 15 more minutes. Drain and rinse in cold water. Quarter potatoes and beets; chill for 1 hour. Prepare dressing by mixing together remaining ingredients. Place potatoes and beets in a serving bowl; toss with the dressing until they are well coated.

Cindy Pierce

Kitchen Tid-Bit:

Slice or cubed, potatoes boiled for salad need to be cooked until they're tender but sill retain their shape. You can ensure a salad that's not mushy by cooking your peeled potatoes this way: Fill a pot with 2 parts water and 1 part vinegar. Add a dash of kosher salt and bring to a boil. Add the potatoes and gently boil them until tender.

LOW-FAT, OLD-FASHIONED POTATO SALAD

1	egg
1	teaspoon red wine vinegar
2	teaspoons fresh lemon juice
1	teaspoon Dijon mustard
3	cloves garlic
1/2	teaspoon salt
1	cup olive oil
2 3/4	pounds Russet potatoes, cooked
3	hard-boiled egg whites
2	hard-boiled eggs
2	stalks celery, finely chopped
1/2	cup white onion, finely chopped
15	ripe black olives, pitted and halved
	Paprika
	Tomato wedges

In blender or food processor, combine egg, vinegar, lemon juice, mustard, garlic and salt to prepare dressing. With machine running, gradually add olive oil, one tablespoon at a time. Chill dressing for at least 4 hours. Meanwhile, cut cooled, cooked potatoes into 1" cubes and cut all egg whites into 1" chunks. Place both into a large salad bowl. Crumble yolks over potatoes. Add celery and onion; chill. Just before serving, toss the potato-egg mixture with desired amount of dressing. Season to taste with salt and pepper. Add olives and paprika; toss. Garnish with tomato wedges.

Lee Harder

MACADAMIA RICE SALAD

2	tablespoons rice vinegar
2	tablespoons vegetable oil
2	cloves garlic, minced
1/2	teaspoon salt
4	cups cooked rice, at room temperature
1/2	cup chopped toasted macadamia nuts
1/2	cup chopped red onion
1/2	cup finely diced celery
1/4	cup chopped celery leaves

Prepare dressing by mixing together vinegar, oil, garlic and salt. Stir dressing into rice, nuts, onion, celery and celery leaves; serve.

Cindy Pierce

Kitchen Tid-Bit:

The trick to turning out perfectly cooked rice lies in completely ignoring the directions on the box. Here's how to do it, regardless of what the directions say: In a saucepan over medium heat, saute the rice in a little oil until the kernels are well coated. Add an amount of water equal to the amount of rice (1 cup to 1 cup, for example). Bring the water to a boil, stir and then reduce the heat to a simmer. Cover and cook for 10 minutes. Remove the pan from the heat and, with the lid still on, let it sit for 15 minutes. Fluff with a fork.

CLASSIC CHICKEN SALAD

3/4	cup mayonnaise
1/2	teaspoon ground ginger
1	tablespoon soy sauce
3	cups cooked chicken, cubed
1/2	cup seedless red or green grapes, cut in half
1	cup celery, diced
1/3	cup sliced green onions
1/2	cup chopped walnuts

Combine mayonnaise, ginger and soy sauce. Stir into remaining ingredients. Cover and chill at least 1 hour. Serve on a bed of mixed salad greens or on bread for sandwiches.

Cindy Sitton

CHICKEN SALAD WITH DATES
AND BLUE CHEESE

4	boneless chicken breasts, whole
1	tablespoon butter
1	green onion, chopped
1	ounce mushrooms, trimmed and chopped
1	slice stale white bread
1/2	ounce blue cheese
3	ounces dates
	Salt and pepper to taste
6	cups salad greens

VINAIGRETTE DRESSING:

1	teaspoon Dijon mustard
	Salt and pepper to taste
2	tablespoons red wine vinegar
1/2	cup olive oil
1	teaspoon sugar

Combine all dressing ingredients and set aside.

Melt butter in a skillet. Add green onion and soften over low heat. Add mushrooms, salt and pepper. Cook over high heat for 2 to 3 minutes until liquid evaporates. Remove from heat.

Crumb bread in a food processor. Add the pitted dates to the bread and lightly process until the dates are chopped. Stir in bread crumb-date mixture and the blue cheese into the green onion-mushroom mixture. Season the stuffing to taste. The stuffing may be made ahead, but do not stuff the chicken until ready to cook.

Make a pocket in each chicken breast and add stuffing evenly to chicken. Place chicken in a buttered baking dish. Cover with buttered foil and bake in a preheated 375° oven for 35 minutes or until no pink juice runs out when you cut into the center of the breast.

Serve the breast hot or cold, cutting them in 4 to 5 diagonal slices and arranging them in a fan on a plate. Toss the greens with half the vinaigrette mixture. Pile the salad on each plate and spoon the remaining dressing over the chicken. Serves 4.

HALEY'S GÁ XÉ PHAY
(SHREDDED CHICKEN SALAD)

2	fresh hot red chilies (e.g. serrano)
3	cloves garlic, minced
2	tablespoons sugar
1	tablespoon rice wine vinegar
3	tablespoons fresh lime juice
3	tablespoons Oriental fish sauce
3	tablespoons vegetable oil
1	pearl onion, thinly sliced
2	cups cooked chicken, shredded
4	cups white cabbage, shredded
2	carrots, peeled and julienned
1/2	cup fresh mint, chopped
	Freshly ground black pepper
	Cilantro

Seed and mince chilies and place in a large bowl (hint: it's a good idea to wear rubber gloves while handling chilies to minimize risk of skin and eye irritation). Add ingredients through and including the pearl onion; mix until sugar dissolves. Add chicken, cabbage, carrots and mint; toss. Season with pepper to taste and serve garnished with cilantro.

Ad Hudler

TURKEY OR CHICKEN SALAD INDIENNE

1	cup cooked poultry meat per person
1/4	cup mayonnaise per cup of meat
1/4	cup coleslaw dressing per cup of meat
1	teaspoon curry powder per cup of dressing
3	mandarin orange sections or 2 grapefruit sections (chopped) per cup of meat
6 to 8	seedless grapes or 1/4 cup white raisins per cup of meat
	Toasted almonds

Poach until done a cut-up turkey or chicken in water, well seasoned with celery and onion. Remove meat from the bones and freeze in a little stock. Separate white and dark meat for future dishes unless the whole bird is needed for the salad. A 20-pound turkey should serve 30 to 35 persons. Let the turkey or chicken thaw overnight. Drain off the stock. Combine the mayonnaise, coleslaw dressing and curry powder. Mix with meat and fruits. Just before serving, sprinkle generously with toasted almonds. Artificial bacon bits and/or grated coconut may be added for additional flavor or for texture. This salad is so good served hot. Bake with nuts on top.

Valerie Williams

MARINATED SHRIMP

3	pounds cooked and cleaned shrimp
1	cup French dressing
1/2	cup chopped green pepper
1/4	cup chopped onion
1/4	cup chopped parsley
1	clove garlic, crushed
2	tablespoons sweet mustard
2	tablespoons lemon juice
	Salt and pepper to taste

Mix all ingredients and chill at least 2 hours.

Mrs. Frederic Comlossy

SANDY'S MACARONI AND TUNA SALAD
(LITTLE TAD LOVES THIS ONE!)

1/4	cup vinegar
2	rounded tablespoons sugar
1	teaspoon Dijon mustard
1	clove garlic, minced
	Salt, pepper and parsley to taste
1	pound hot cooked macaroni
1	small onion, chopped
3 to 4	cloves garlic, minced
1	large can white meat tuna (may substitute shrimp or chicken)
1/2	package frozen peas
1/3	cup mayonnaise
	Hard-boiled egg slices and parsley as garnish

Prepare dressing by mixing together vinegar, sugar, Dijon mustard, garlic and seasonings. In a serving bowl, combine macaroni, onion, garlic, tuna and frozen peas. Stir in dressing and chill until cold. Just before serving, toss with mayonnaise. Garnish with hard-boiled eggs and parsley.

Sandy Caldwell

Notes

EAT YOUR VEGGIES

Good-for-You (and Great-Tasting, too!)
Main and Side Dishes

ROASTED ASPARAGUS

2   bunches asparagus, tough ends trimmed
1   red pepper, sliced
3   cloves garlic, sliced
1   small onion, sliced
     Olive oil
     Salt and pepper to taste

Preheat oven to 500°. Combine first 4 ingredients in a roasting pan and toss with olive oil to coat. Season with salt and pepper. Roast for 20 minutes.

NOTE: Leftovers, if there happens to be any, are great served straight from the refrigerator.

Cindy Pierce

BROCCOLI BAKE

2	10-ounce boxes frozen, chopped broccoli, thawed
1	medium onion, finely chopped
1	cup Bisquick
4	eggs, lightly beaten
1/2	cup vegetable oil
1	cup grated extra sharp Cheddar cheese
1	tablespoon chopped fresh parsley
	Salt and pepper to taste

Mix all ingredients together and blend well. Pour into oiled baking pan. Bake at 350° for 35 to 40 minutes, until top is light brown.

Twink Underhill
Original proprietor, The Unpressured Cooker

Quotable Kid:

You can't hide a piece of broccoli in a glass of milk.
Sachelle, 6

ROASTED BROCCOLI
WITH LEMON-GARLIC BATH

1	head broccoli (about 1 pound)
2	cloves garlic, smashed and peeled
1	teaspoon kosher salt
	Freshly ground black pepper to taste
1/4	cup fresh lemon juice
1/4	cup olive oil

Using a vegetable peeler, peel the entire length of the broccoli stem. Slice lengthwise into 9 to 10 pieces, with 2" wide strips at the floret end. Heat oven to 500° with a rack placed on the lowest level of the oven. Place broccoli pieces into a 14x12x2" roasting pan. Smash garlic cloves with salt and pepper into a paste, using a mortar and pestle or by pressing the garlic with the back of a knife onto a cutting board. Put lemon juice into a small bowl and add garlic paste, whisking until smooth. Blend in olive oil. Pour mixture evenly over broccoli and stir to coat all of the sides. Roast for 7 minutes. Turn and continue roasting for 8 more minutes. Broccoli is done when the stem is easily pierced with a sharp knife. Remove pieces that are done and continue roasting remaining pieces for 5 to 10 more minutes. May be served heated or at room temperature. Broccoli may also be reheated in a 500° oven for approximately 7 minutes. Yields 2 to 4 as first course or side dish.

Kevin Pierce

BLANCHED BROCCOLI
WITH SESAME VINAIGRETTE

1	large head broccoli, cut into florets (or approximately 1 pound fresh cut florets)

VINAIGRETTE:

1	tablespoon vegetable oil
1	tablespoon soy sauce
1	tablespoon sesame oil
1	teaspoon salt (optional)
1	clove crushed garlic
2	tablespoons toasted sesame seeds

Blanch broccoli in boiling salted water or steam lightly. Broccoli should be crunchy. Place in large Ziploc bag. Prepare vinaigrette and add to broccoli in Ziploc bag; shake. Marinate for 1 to 2 hours prior to serving. Broccoli may be served cold or at room temperature.

Linda Wener

SWEET AND SOUR RED CABBAGE

5	cups shredded red cabbage
2	tablespoons brown sugar
1/2	cup water
1	teaspoon salt
1	small onion, sliced
4	slices bacon
2	tablespoons flour
1/3	cup vinegar
1/8	teaspoon pepper

Cook cabbage in 1/2 cup water with 1/2 teaspoon salt for 5 to 8 minutes or until crisp tender; drain. Fry bacon; remove bacon and half of fat, stir in flour to remaining bacon fat in skillet. Add water, brown sugar, vinegar, salt and pepper and onion. Cook until thick, add bacon and cabbage. Heat through and serve. Good with roast beef or pork. Makes 6 servings.

Jennie Steenhuis

POTATOES AND ONIONS PROVENCALE
(GRILLED FOR JAMIE)

3	pounds all-purpose potatoes
2	onions
1/4	cup olive oil
1	tablespoon lemon juice
2	tablespoons chopped parsley
2	tablespoons capers
1	garlic clove, crushed in press
1/2	teaspoon salt
1/4	teaspoon pepper

Peel potatoes and cut into slices 1/2" thick. Cut onions into thin wedges. Mix potatoes and onions with olive oil, lemon juice, parsley, capers, garlic, salt and pepper. Prepare 6-18" long strips of aluminum foil. Place potatoes and onions on each of the sheets and seal edges to make 6 flat, closed packages. Grill over low heat for approximately 1 hour, until potatoes are tender. Turn occasionally. Pierce a hole in each packet to let stem escape before serving. Yields 6 servings.

Kas Chenciner

SID'S HORSERADISH SMASHED POTATOES

3	pounds baking potatoes, cut into 1" chunks
1/3	cup butter or margarine
3/4	cup half and half
1	teaspoon salt
1 to 2	tablespoons freshly grated horseradish (or 2 to 4 tablespoons prepared horseradish)

Place potatoes in water to cover and boil over medium-high heat 20 minutes or until tender; drain. Mash potatoes with an electric mixer at medium speed. Add butter, half and half, salt and horseradish; beat until fluffy. Yields 8 servings.

Danny Mellman

PERFECT MASHED POTATOES

2	pounds Idaho potatoes, peeled and quartered (<u>must</u> be Idaho!)
2	teaspoons kosher salt
8	tablespoons (1 stick) unsalted butter
1/2	cup heavy cream
1/2	cup milk
1/4	teaspoon freshly ground white pepper

Place potatoes in a 2-quart saucepan with 1 teaspoon of the salt and add cold water to cover. Bring to a boil, lower heat and simmer for about 30 minutes, covered, until potatoes are tender. Drain well for several minutes. Mix together the butter, heavy cream and milk in another saucepan and heat over low heat until butter has melted; keep warm. Add butter and milk to potatoes, using a food mill or ricer to mash.

NOTE: Avoid the use of a hand-held masher, which gives lumpy potatoes, and a food processor, which makes them gummy and tough.

Kevin Pierce

B-B-Q POTATOES WITH GARLIC AND ROSEMARY

Easy to prepare, nothing to clean up and absolutely delicious alongside any grilled meat or chicken.

10	small new potatoes
2	cloves garlic, thinly sliced
1 1/3	teaspoons ground rosemary
1/3	cup olive oil
	Salt and pepper to taste

Wash the potatoes very well and cut into quarters. Put the cut potatoes, sliced garlic, rosemary, salt and pepper in a large bowl. Drizzle the olive oil over the ingredients and mix well. Cut 2-18" lengths of good quality foil. Put half the potato mixture on each length of foil. Seal the 2 parcels very well so that no juices escape during cooking. Preheat the grill. Cook the foil packets directly on the grill for 10 minutes over low-medium heat. Flip the packets carefully and continue cooking until the potatoes are tender (about 10 to 15 minutes).

MALLOW WHIPPED SWEET POTATOES

4	cups hot mashed sweet potatoes
1/4	cup margarine
1/4	cup orange juice
1/4	teaspoon salt
1	cup miniature marshmallows

Combine the mashed sweet potatoes with margarine and orange juice. Add salt and whip in the miniature marshmallows. Place in 1 1/2-quart casserole and bake at 350° for 20 minutes. If frozen, allow 1 1/4 hours at 375°. Makes 8 generous servings.

Van Hooper

MASHED SWEET POTATOES
WITH BALSAMIC VINEGAR

4 to 5	large sweet potatoes (4 pounds), scrubbed
2	tablespoons butter
1/8	teaspoon ground cinnamon
1/8	teaspoon freshly grated nutmeg
1	cup milk
1	teaspoon salt
	Freshly ground black pepper
1 to 2	teaspoons balsamic vinegar

Preheat oven to 400°. Bake sweet potatoes in oven for 50 minutes or until easily pierced. Cool until potatoes can be handled. Remove skin and press through a ricer or food mill; set aside. Heat butter over low heat until brown. Add cinnamon and nutmeg; remove from heat. Add milk, return to heat and bring milk to a boil. Stir in the sweet potato puree and mix thoroughly. Add salt, pepper and balsamic vinegar to taste. Yields 4 servings.

Kevin Pierce

ALYSSA'S SUNFLOWER RICE

2 to 4	tablespoons unsalted butter
1	cup brown rice
3	tablespoons grated Parmesan cheese
1/4	cup sunflower seed kernels
	Salt to taste
2 1/2	cups chicken broth

Melt the butter in a medium saucepan over medium heat. Add the rice to the melted butter and stir with a wooden spoon until each grain of rice glistens with butter. Pour chicken broth over the rice, stir once. Let mixture come to a boil. Turn heat down to very low. Cover the saucepan and let simmer until the rice is tender and has absorbed all the broth, about 50 minutes. Turn off the heat and remove saucepan from stove. Add the Parmesan cheese and sunflower seeds. Stir lightly. If you want a richer dish, add up to 2 tablespoons more butter. Add salt to taste. Serves 4 to 6.

Diana Perez

ROYALTY RICE

3   cups coconut milk
1   teaspoon salt
1   cup rice

During World War II, while stationed in new Guinea, I learned from a native that the most favorite food was polished rice cooked in coconut milk. It is also a choice food for me. The recipe is to boil rice as usual, but use coconut milk. Bring coconut milk to a boil, put in the salt and rice, boil 10 minutes, simmer 20 minutes.

NOTE: If some is leftover, make a rice pudding. Beat an egg, add some sugar and milk, mix in the rice and bake.

"Uncle Joe" Wightman

SAUTEED SPINACH WITH GARLIC

2	pounds fresh spinach
1	garlic clove, peeled
3	tablespoons extra-virgin olive oil
1/8	teaspoon kosher salt
	Freshly ground black pepper
1	lemon, quartered (optional)

Remove stems from spinach leaves and discard leaves that are discolored or tough. Wash spinach thoroughly in cold water to dislodge sand and grit. Dry spinach in a salad spinner or on paper towels. Or avoid necessity of cleaning spinach by buying jet-washed, ready-to-use spinach in the "gourmet greens" section of produce market.

Heat olive oil over high heat in a large saucepan or skillet and add spinach. Stab the prongs of a dinner fork into a clove of garlic and use the garlic-stuck fork to stir spinach quickly and continually. Cook for 3 to 4 minutes until spinach is wilted and season with salt and pepper to taste. Continue to cook for 1 to 2 minutes longer until spinach is tender. Serve hot or at room temperature. Just before serving, splash spinach with lemon juice.

Cindy Pierce

SQUASH CASSEROLE

	Squash or zucchini
1/4	cup sour cream
	Thyme
1	egg
	Parmesan cheese

Cook about 3 cups of squash, cut up. Drain well and add beaten egg, sour cream, Parmesan cheese to taste, salt and generous sprinklings of thyme. Top with buttered bread crumbs and bake at 350° for 30 to 40 minutes.

Susie Santamaria

Kitchen Tid-Bit:

For carrots that taste like carrots, don't peel them before you boil them. Simply wash them and cook them with the skin on, in salted boiling water. Once they are soft enough to pierce with a fork, plunge them into cold water. The peel will rub right off, leaving behind their distinctive "carroty" taste.

CRUSTY PECAN SQUASH

2	12-ounce packages frozen squash
1/3	cup melted butter
1/3	cup evaporated milk or cream
2	tablespoons brown sugar
1	teaspoon salt
1/2	teaspoon nutmeg
1/2	teaspoon pepper
1/2	cup coarsely broken pecans
2	tablespoons corn syrup, light or dark

Thaw squash. Preheat oven to 400°. In large bowl, combine thawed squash, melted butter, milk, brown sugar, salt, pepper and nutmeg. Turn into greased 1 1/2-quart casserole. In small bowl, combine pecans and corn syrup. Sprinkle these over squash in casserole. Bake 30 minutes. Makes 6 servings.

Martha Ryckman
First director of the Children's Center

OVEN ROASTED TOMATOES

12	ripe plum tomatoes, halved lengthwise
2	tablespoons olive oil, divided
	Salt and pepper to taste
1/4	cup fresh parsley, chopped
1 1/2	teaspoons fresh thyme, chopped
1	clove garlic, crushed

Preheat oven to 425°. Line a shallow baking dish with foil for ease of clean up. Place tomatoes in dish, cut side up. Drizzle with 1 tablespoon of the olive oil. Season liberally with salt and pepper. Roast for about 1 hour, until tomatoes are shriveled and beginning to brown on the bottom. Meanwhile, in a small bowl, mix parsley, thyme, garlic and remaining 1 tablespoon of oil. Remove tomatoes from oven and sprinkle herb mixture evenly over the top. Return to the oven for 15 minutes or until herbs are slightly browned. Serve at room temperature.

Nancy Gerhard

ZUCCHINI FRITTATA

6 to 8	small zucchini or other small summer squash (8 cups after shredding)
8	eggs
	Bit of pepper
3	tablespoons cooking oil
1	teaspoon salt
1/2	cup grated Parmesan cheese

Shred squash coarsely into small towel and twist to extract as much liquid as possible. Heat oil in large, broiler-proof skillet. Add squash and cook slowly about 5 minutes or until just tender. Beat eggs with salt and pepper; pour over squash. Cook until just set, stirring gently. Sprinkle cheese on top and put under broiler to brown. Cut in wedges to serve. Makes 6 to 8 servings.

Vera Swanson

ROASTED VEGETABLES

Potatoes, diced
Carrots, diced
Turnips, diced
Zucchini, diced
Onions, diced
Garlic, sliced thin
Salt and pepper
Olive oil

Dice vegetables of your choice into 1 to 1 1/2" pieces. Mix lightly with olive oil. Lay out on a cookie sheet and sprinkle with garlic, salt and pepper. Roast at 400° until crisp tender.

Sharon Chamberlain

PROVENCAL VEGETABLES
WITH GOAT CHEESE

1/4	pound broccoli florets
1/4	pound green beans
1/4	pound snow peas
2	small zucchini, cut into thick slices
2 1/2	ounces goat cheese
2	large garlic cloves
4	tablespoons olive oil
1	tablespoon fresh lemon juice
	Pinch of dried thyme
4 to 5	ripe, juicy tomatoes, coarsely chopped
	Salt and fresh ground black pepper
	to taste
2	scallions, minced
	Pinenuts for garnish

In a large pot of boiling salted water, blanch the vegetables in batches until just tender but still very firm to the bite: 6 to 7 minutes for the broccoli, 5 minutes for the beans and 2 to 3 minutes for the snow peas and zucchini. Drain each batch of vegetables promptly as they are ready and refresh them under cold water. Drain well, pat dry and let cool.

DRESSING: Put the cheese, garlic, oil, lemon juice and thyme in a blender or food processor and mix until smooth. Add the tomatoes in small batches, processing each until smooth. Add just enough to give the dressing a rich consistency that is thick but liquid enough to coat the vegetables; season well. Put the cooled vegetables in a large bowl and pour the dressing over all. Toss well to coat all the ingredients thoroughly. Scatter the scallions and pinenuts over the top before serving. Serves 4.

Tina Bryan

GRILLED VEGETABLE KABOBS WITH RICE

1/2	cup prepared oil-free Italian dressing
1	tablespoon minced fresh parsley or
	1 teaspoon dried parsley flakes
1	teaspoon dried whole basil
2	medium size yellow squash, cut into
	1" slices
8	small boiling onions
8	cherry tomatoes
8	medium size fresh mushrooms
	Vegetable cooking spray
2	cups hot cooked long grain rice

Mix dressing, parsley and basil in a small bowl, cover and refrigerate. Place squash, onions, tomatoes and mushrooms in an alternating sequence on 8 skewers. Apply cooking spray to grill rack and place on grill over medium heat. Position kabobs on rack and cook until vegetables are tender, about 15 minutes. Baste with dressing mixture and turn skewers frequently. Serve 2 vegetable kabobs on top of 1/2 cup of rice per plate.

BLACK BEAN BURGERS

3	16-ounce cans black beans, rinsed and drained
1 1/2	cups uncooked regular oats
1	medium onion, diced
2	jalapeno peppers, seeded and diced
3/4	cup chopped fresh cilantro
2	large eggs, lightly beaten
1	teaspoon salt
1/4	cup all-purpose flour
1/4	cup cornmeal
1	tablespoon vegetable oil
8	hamburger buns

Mash beans coarsely. Add oats, peppers, cilantro, eggs and salt to the beans; mix and shape into 8 patties. Blend flour and cornmeal; dredge patties in the mixture. Heat oil in large non-stick skillet over medium-high heat; add patties. Cook for 5 minutes on each side or until lightly browned. Drain on paper towels and serve on buns. Patties may be garnished with tomato slices, fresh cilantro leaves and jalapeno peppers. Yields 8 servings.

THREE-GRAIN CASSEROLE

2	tablespoons butter or margarine
1/3	cup pearl barley
1/3	cup brown rice
1	cup chopped celery
1/2	cup chopped onion
4	cups boiling water
1/2	teaspoon salt
1/3	cup white rice
4	dried apricots, chopped
1/2	cup halved cherry tomatoes

Melt butter or margarine. Add barley, brown rice, celery and onion. Cook and stir until onions are tender, about 10 minutes. Add water and salt. Cover and cook for 25 minutes; add white rice. Cook until all grains are tender and water is absorbed, about 15 to 20 minutes. Stir in apricots. Add cherry tomatoes just before serving. Serve immediately or chill and serve cold. Serves 6.

Tina Bryan

SOUTHERN CORN PUDDING

3 eggs, well beaten
3 tablespoons sifted flour
2 teaspoons salt
1 tablespoon sugar
1 tablespoon melted butter
1 can cream style corn
2 cups whole milk, scalded

Butter 4x8" Pyrex casserole dish. Beat eggs well. Add flour, salt, sugar and melted butter to beaten eggs. Add corn and scalded milk. If milk is not scalded, a longer baking time will be needed. Bake at 350° for 40 minutes or until a knife inserted in edge of pudding comes out clean.

NOTE: The center of the pudding will be soft, but it will continue to thicken upon standing.

Evelyn Pearson

PUFFED CHEESE GRITS

2	tablespoons butter
1/4	cup onion, chopped
2	cups water
1/2	teaspoon salt
1/2	cup quick grits
1	teaspoon Tabasco
	Freshly ground black pepper
1 3/4	cups grated Cheddar cheese
3	tablespoons soft butter
2	egg whites, beaten stiff

Melt 2 tablespoons butter in frying pan and saute onions 4 to 5 minutes until translucent. Bring water to boil, add salt and pour in grits slowly. Boil, stirring constantly. Reduce heat and cook until thick. Add onions, Tabasco, pepper, 1 1/2 cups cheese and butter to the grits. Stir together until cheese melts. Grease 1-quart souffle dish. Beat egg whites until stiff peak stage. Gently and thoroughly fold egg whites into the cheese-grits mixture. Pour into dish and sprinkle the rest of the cheese on top. Bake for 30 minutes at 400° until puffed and brown. Makes 4 to 6 servings.

NOTE: A yummy change from rice or potatoes.

Mariel Goss
Co-chair, 1st edition
Sanibel-Captiva Cookbook

MOCK CHEESE SOUFFLE

1	loaf French bread, diced
1	pound grated sharp cheese
4	eggs
3 to 4	cups milk
1/2	teaspoon dry mustard
1/2	teaspoon salt
	Paprika

Spread half of bread cubes on bottom of lightly greased baking dish. Add some of the cheese. Repeat a layer of bread and cheese. Whip eggs and add the milk, mustard and salt. Pour over bread and cheese. Sprinkle top with paprika. Make a collar around top of casserole with foil about 2" high. Bake, uncovered, at 350° for an hour or until knife inserted into center comes out clean. Makes 8 to 10 servings.

Evelyn Neale

BAKED CHEESE GRITS

3	cups water
1/2	teaspoon salt
1	cup instant grits
1	cup milk
3/4	cup grated sharp Cheddar cheese
1/2	stick butter, cut in small pieces
2	eggs, beaten
1	garlic clove, minced

Butter shallow 2-quart baking dish. Bring water and salt to boil over high heat. Gradually whisk in the grits, stirring to prevent lumps. Blend in milk, half of the cheese, butter and garlic. Remove from stove and whisk in the beaten eggs rapidly, stirring well. Sprinkle the rest of the cheese on the top; refrigerate. Preheat oven to 350° and bake until grits are set, generally about 40 minutes. Serve hot.

Notes

WHAT'S FOR SUPPER?

Everybody's Favorite Entrees
with Pasta, Beef, Pork and Poultry

LOW-FAT MACARONI AND CHEESE

4	cups cooked elbow macaroni (2 cups uncooked)
2	cups shredded, reduced-fat Cheddar cheese
1	cup low-fat cottage cheese
3/4	cup nonfat sour cream
1/2	cup skim milk
2	tablespoons grated fresh onion
1 1/2	teaspoons reduced-calorie stick margarine, melted
1/2	teaspoon salt
1/4	teaspoon pepper
1	egg, lightly beaten
	Vegetable cooking spray
1/4	cup dry bread crumbs
1	tablespoon reduced-calorie stick margarine, melted
1/4	teaspoon paprika
	Fresh oregano sprigs

Coat a 2-quart casserole with cooking spray. Mix together first 10 ingredients (up through egg) and put into casserole. Blend bread crumbs, margarine and paprika; sprinkle on top of casserole. Bake, covered, for 30 minutes at 350°. Uncover and bake for 5 minutes or until set. Garnish with oregano. Yields 6 servings.

Cindy Pierce

GRANDMA'S TAMALE PIE

2	tablespoons olive oil
1/2	cup each: diced onion, green and red pepper
1	jalapeno pepper, seeded and chopped
1	large clove garlic, chopped
1	teaspoon each chili powder and salt
1/2	teaspoon each paprika and ground cumin
1/4	teaspoon each cayenne and black pepper
1	8-ounce can whole corn kernels, drained
2	cups milk
2	cups water
1	cup yellow cornmeal
1	cup grated Cheddar cheese
1/4	cup chopped cilantro

Preheat oven to 400°. Heat oil over medium heat in a cast-iron skillet. Add onion, peppers and garlic. Cook for 3 to 4 minutes until onion is translucent and peppers are softened. Add spices and cook, stirring, for 1 minute. Add corn, milk and water; bring mixture to a boil. Stir in cornmeal gradually. When mixture returns to boil, reduce heat to low and stir occasionally for about 25 minutes or until mixture thickens. Remove from heat and let cool completely. Top with grated cheese and bake for 10 to 15 minutes. Garnish with chopped cilantro.

Helen Pierce

PASTA WITH CHICKEN, BROCCOLI AND MARINATED MUSHROOMS

1/4	cup olive oil
1	clove garlic, minced
3	skinless, boneless chicken breasts, cut into bite size chunks
2	tablespoons fresh oregano
2	tablespoons soy sauce
1	cup dry white wine
1	bunch broccoli, cut into florets, with stem discarded
1	16-ounce jar marinated Italian mushrooms, drained and quartered
8	tablespoons (1 stick) butter
2	pounds fresh spaghetti
2	cups freshly grated Romano cheese
1/2	cup Italian-style dried bread crumbs
	Freshly ground black pepper to taste

Warm the olive oil in a large skillet over medium-high heat. Add garlic and cook for a few minutes. When it is translucent, add chicken pieces and cook until they are browned. Add oregano, soy sauce and wine. Lower heat to a simmer and continue cooking for 2 minutes. Add broccoli and cover the pan with a tightly fitting lid. Steam for 3 to 5 minutes. Add mushrooms and steam for another 2 minutes in a covered pan. Add butter one tablespoon at a time, making sure each tablespoon is melted before adding the next. Set pan aside, covered. Cook pasta according to package directions and drain. To serve, mix together half of the chicken, half of the cheese and half of the bread crumbs. Stir in the spaghetti and add pepper to taste. Top with the other half of the chicken, cheese and bread crumbs.

Kevin Pierce

BAKED ZITI WITH SPINACH AND CHEESE

1	16-ounce package ziti
2	10-ounce packages frozen chopped spinach
1	15-ounce carton ricotta cheese
3	large eggs
2/3	cup grated Parmesan cheese
1/4	teaspoon ground pepper
1	27 1/2-ounce can spaghetti sauce
2	teaspoons dried oregano
1	12-ounce package shredded mozzarella cheese

Preheat oven to 375°. Cook ziti and spinach according to package directions. Mix together drained spinach, ricotta cheese, eggs, Parmesan cheese and pepper in a large bowl. Add spaghetti sauce and oregano to the drained ziti. Layer half of the pasta mixture in a 12x8x2" glass baking dish and top with spinach and mozzarella cheese. Repeat with a second layer of pasta and sauce. Cover the baking dish with foil and bake for 25 minutes. Remove foil and bake for another 5 minutes. Cool for 10 minutes before serving.

Mary Beth Greenplate

HATTIE'S MOM'S PASTA PUTTANESCA

1/4	cup olive oil
1	tin anchovies
3 to 4	garlic cloves, chopped
	Pinch of red pepper flakes
1	small can chopped black olives (or, if you can find them, imported Nicoise olives, pitted and chopped - - it's worth the effort!)
1	28-ounce can imported Italian tomatoes, drained and chopped
1	3-ounce jar capers
1	pound pasta (spaghetti or rigatoni is best)
1	small can minced clams (optional)

Heat the olive oil over medium-high in a large, deep skillet or Dutch oven. Add the anchovies and chopped garlic to the oil, smash with fork until anchovies are paste. Add remaining ingredients except pasta and cook, covered, over low heat, for at least 30 minutes (the longer you simmer, the richer the sauce). Serve over cooked pasta.

NOTE: If you opt for the clams, add them just before serving so they don't get tough.

Cindy Pierce

Kitchen Tid-Bit:

Here's a smashing way to peel garlic: Place the head of garlic on the counter and press on the root end to loosen the cloves. Separate a clove from the head and set it on a cutting board. Lay the flat side of a chef's knife on the clove and press down firmly until the clove snaps. Pick up the clove and the peel will come right off.

MILLION-DOLLAR SPAGHETTI

1	package thin spaghetti
1 1/2	pounds ground beef
8	ounces cream cheese
1/3	cup scallions, chopped
	Ground pepper
1	tablespoon butter
2	8-ounce cans tomato sauce
1/4	cup sour cream
1/2	pound cottage cheese

Cook spaghetti and drain. Cook beef in butter until brown and add tomato sauce. Combine cheeses, sour cream and scallions. Layer spaghetti and cheese mixture in casserole dish. Pour tomato and beef over the top. Chill until ready to cook. Bake at 350° for 45 minutes. Makes 6 to 8 servings.

Mariel Goss
Co-chair, 1st edition
Sanibel-Captiva Cookbook

KENDALL'S SPINACH AND TOFU LASAGNA

12	ounces firm tofu, drained
4	tablespoons lemon juice
2 1/2	tablespoons almond butter (peanut butter may be substituted)
1	tablespoon low-sodium soy sauce
1	tablespoon extra-virgin olive oil
1	large yellow onion, diced
2	large cloves garlic, pressed
	Freshly ground pepper
1	teaspoon oregano
1	teaspoon basil
1/2	pound fresh mushrooms, sliced 1/4" thick
1/2	cup dry sherry or nonalcoholic wine
2	packages frozen chopped spinach, thawed and squeezed dry
1/2	cup fresh parsley, finely chopped
1/4	cup fine bread crumbs, lightly toasted
1/2	cup toasted walnuts, chopped
4	cups tomato sauce
9	lasagna noodles, cooked al dente
	Grated Parmesan cheese

Puree tofu in a food processor or blender. Blend in lemon juice, almond butter and soy sauce until smooth. Add olive oil to large, nonstick skillet or Dutch oven that has been warmed over medium heat. When the oil is hot, add onion and saute for a few minutes. Add garlic, pepper, oregano, basil and mushrooms and saute until mushrooms are softened. Stir in the sherry, spinach, parsley and saute for a few more minutes. Add vegetables to the tofu and blend the mixture so that it is still slightly chunky. Preheat oven to 350°. Oil a 9x13" baking dish and spread half of the bread crumbs across the bottom and sides of the dish. Place approximately 1/3 of the walnuts on top of the bread crumbs and next one cup of the tomato sauce. Place 3 lasagna noodles side-by-side on top. Add half of the tofu mixture. Repeat, with two more layerings of walnuts, sauce, noodles and tofu. Add the remaining tomato sauce and shake remaining bread crumbs on top. Sprinkle with Parmesan cheese, cover and bake for 30 minutes. Uncover and bake for 10 more minutes. Cool for 20 to 30 minutes before serving. Yields 8 servings.

Leslie Cook

VEGETARIAN LASAGNA

1	pound lasagna noodles, uncooked
1	tablespoon margarine
1/2	cup onion, chopped
2	cloves garlic, crushed
2	tablespoons sugar
1	teaspoon fresh basil, chopped
1/4	teaspoon black pepper
1	28-ounce can whole tomatoes, cut up, not drained
2	8-ounce cans tomato paste
1/2	cup water
1	egg, slightly beaten
1	15-ounce container low-fat ricotta cheese
1	pound mozzarella cheese, grated
3	teaspoons fresh parsley, chopped
1	cup grated Parmesan cheese

Saute onion in oil. Add garlic, sugar, basil and pepper. Stir in cut-up tomatoes with liquid. Add tomato paste and water. Simmer for 30 minutes.

Combine egg, ricotta, parsley and mozzarella in a large mixing bowl.

Line bottom of 9x13" baking dish with 1 cup of prepared tomato sauce. Lay 3 uncooked lasagna pieces on top, then alternate with 1/3 of the sauce, 1/3 of the ricotta mixture. Repeat layers, sprinkle top with Parmesan cheese. Cover and bake at 375° for 30 minutes. Uncover and bake 20 minutes longer.

Nancy Gerhard

SALLY'S BIG SECRET LASAGNA

1/4	cup olive oil
1	pound ground beef
1	cup chopped onion
2	cloves garlic, finely chopped
1	28-ounce can Italian plum tomatoes
2	6-ounce cans tomato paste
2	teaspoons salt
1	teaspoon dried basil
1/2	teaspoon dried oregano
1/4	teaspoon black pepper
1	cup ripe olives, cut in quarters
8	ounces lasagna noodles
1	bay leaf
1/2	pound sliced mozzarella cheese
1/2	cup freshly grated Parmesan cheese
1	carton ricotta cheese (small curd cottage cheese may be substituted)

Heat olive oil in heavy skillet. Add ground beef and cook until browned. Add chopped onion and garlic; cook until transparent. Add the plum tomatoes (crush the tomatoes with your hands as they are added to the pan), tomato paste, salt, basil, oregano, black pepper and bay leaf. Cover and simmer for 1 hour, until sauce is thickened. Stir in the quartered olives.

While sauce simmers, cook lasagna noodles in boiling, salted water until tender, about 20 minutes. Drain lasagna. Spread about 1/4 of sauce in shallow baking dish. Cover with a layer of lasagna, arranging strips lengthwise in dish. Add layer of mozzarella cheese using about half, then layer of Parmesan cheese. Put carton of ricotta cheese in middle and repeat layers ending with sauce and Parmesan cheese. Bake at 350° for 40 to 50 minutes. Serve with garlic bread and tossed salad.

Sally Dekold

TURKEY TETRAZZINI

1/2	pound linguine
	Salt
1/2	pound mushrooms, sliced
1 1/2	cups turkey stock
1/2	cup heavy cream
3	cups cooked cold turkey, 1" diced
2	tablespoons dry bread crumbs
10	tablespoons butter
	Fresh ground white or black pepper
4	tablespoons flour
1	egg yolk
1	tablespoon Madeira
1/4	cup freshly grated Parmesan

Preheat oven to 350°. Drop the linguine into at least 4 quarts boiling salted water and cook until it is slightly resistant to the teeth, about 9 minutes. Drain, lifting with 2 forks to rid all lurking water. Put in large mixing bowl. Stir into it 2 tablespoons of the butter and season highly with salt and pepper.

Melt 3 tablespoons butter in frypan. When the foam subsides, stir in the mushrooms. Cook briefly over high heat, turning with a wooden spoon, for 2 to 3 minutes. Do not brown. Place in small bowl. Melt 3 more tablespoons of the butter in the same pan and stir in (off the heat) the flour. Mix it to a paste and add (all at once) the stock. Return pan to heat and stir with wire whisk. Slowly bring sauce to a boil, cook until it is smooth and thick. Simmer 5 minutes.

In a small bowl, mix together the egg yolk and cream. Stir in 2 tablespoons of the simmering sauce. Now pour the cream mixture into the pan of sauce. Season sauce highly with salt and a little white pepper. Add 1 tablespoon Madeira and fold in the mushrooms and diced turkey.

Butter a 1 1/2-quart casserole and put in half of the pasta. Cover this with half of the turkey mixture, then spread over it the remaining pasta. Spoon the rest of the turkey mixture over the top and sprinkle it evenly with the combined cheese and crumbs. Dot all over with bits of butter. Bake in preheated oven until bubbly and top begins to brown. If necessary, pass it briefly under the broiler to brown a little more.

NOTE: The 1 1/2 cups turkey stock can be part turkey gravy and part canned chicken stock, or all chicken stock.

Alice MacKenzie

THAI SURPRISE

6 ounces uncooked rice noodles or
  vermicelli (thin spaghetti)
5 tablespoons soy sauce
2 tablespoons peanut butter
1 tablespoon brown sugar
3 tablespoons peanut oil
3 eggs, beaten
6 scallions, cut in 1" lengths
1 pound fresh mung bean sprouts
3 cloves garlic, crushed
  Up to 1 1/2 tablespoons crushed red
  pepper
1 pound firm tofu, cut in small cubes
1/3 cup cider vinegar
1 1/2 cups chopped toasted peanuts
  Wedges of lime

Cook noodles 3 to 5 minutes in boiling water or as stated on box in case of vermicelli. Drain and rinse in cold running water, drain thoroughly; set aside.

Combine soy sauce, peanut butter and brown sugar in small bowl. Stir until it forms a paste and set aside.

Heat a large skillet or wok. Add 1 tablespoon oil. Wait 1 minute, then add beaten eggs. Cook until eggs are dry. Remove and set aside.

Heat wok again. Add 2 tablespoons oil, scallions, bean sprouts, garlic and red pepper. Stir-fry for a minute. Add tofu; stir-fry a few more minutes. Add cooked noodles to skillet. Stir-fry, combining everything as uniformly as possible, about 5 more minutes. Add peanut butter paste, along with vinegar. Stir and cook several more minutes. Stir in cooked egg. Serve immediately, topped with peanuts and wedges of lime.

Liz Fowler

AMARETTO CHICKEN

2 to 3	tablespoons butter or vegetable oil
5	boneless, skinless chicken breasts, cut into medallions
1/4	cup bread crumbs
1	ounce sliced roasted almonds
1/2	cup flour
1	egg, beaten
1	quart heavy cream
2	cups apple juice
4	tablespoons cornstarch
2	ounces water
1	ounce green onions, chopped
1	cup seedless grapes
1 1/2	ounces Amaretto
1	teaspoon sugar
	Cooked rice
1	teaspoon white pepper
1	large apple, cut in thin strips

Melt butter or oil in a large frying pan. Combine bread crumbs and almonds in a small bowl. Dredge chicken breasts in flour, then beaten egg and finally in bread crumb mixture. Saute approximately 1 1/2 minutes, until golden brown.

To make sauce, combine white pepper, heavy cream and apple juice in a saucepan. Heat until boiling, stirring frequently. Mix cornstarch and water until very smooth. Add to sauce and stir until thickened. Add green onion, grapes, Amaretto, sliced apple and sugar. Serve chicken over rice and lace with the Amaretto cream sauce.

Noopie Khemkhajon

BRAISED CHICKEN

1	frying chicken, quartered
	Salt and pepper
1/4	pound mushrooms, sliced
1	tablespoon flour
3	tablespoons butter
1	medium onion, thinly sliced
1/4	cup dry white wine
1	cup light cream

Brown chicken in butter, season with salt and pepper. Remove from pan, add onion and mushrooms. Cook about 5 minutes. Add chicken and wine. Cover and simmer 45 minutes or until chicken is tender. Remove chicken from pan. Add cream and flour to remaining sauce and simmer a few minutes. Serve sauce over chicken.

Margaret Ernest

WORLD'S BEST (AND EASIEST!) ROASTED CHICKEN

1   6- to 7-pound roasting chicken
1   lemon (optional)
     Kosher salt
     Fresh ground pepper

Preheat the oven to 500°. Cut the lemon in half and put both slices in the bird's cavity. Put the bird in a roasting pan. Rub with kosher salt and fresh ground pepper. Put the pan in the oven and roast for 20 minutes per pound. That's it! No kidding!

Kevin Pierce

YUMMY CHICKEN

1	3- to 4-pound cut-up frying chicken or 2 to 3 chicken breasts, halved and boned
1/4	cup honey (orange blossom preferred)
1/4	cup dry sherry
1/4	cup soy sauce
1	teaspoon seasoned salt

Combine honey, soy sauce, sherry and salt. Place the chicken pieces in a shallow baking pan and pour over them the marinade. Marinate several hours, turning the chicken occasionally. Bake at 350° until browned and tender, about 1 to 1 1/2 hours.

Harriet Howe

GRANDMA PIERCE'S CHICKEN CASSEROLE

4	chicken breasts, cooked
6	slices white bread, torn into small pieces
2	eggs, beaten
1	10-ounce can mushroom soup, undiluted
2	10-ounce cans chicken noodle soup, undiluted
1	3- to 4-ounce can mushroom stems and pieces, drained
1/2	stick (4 tablespoons) butter
1/2	cup corn flake crumbs or bread crumbs

Break cooked chicken into small pieces. Combine with bread, eggs, soups and mushrooms and place in 9x13" greased pan. Melt 1/2 stick butter and toss with 1/2 cup corn flake or bread crumbs. Sprinkle over top and bake at 375° for 1 hour.

Kristy Applegate

TROPICAL CHICKEN

8	skinless, boneless chicken breast halves
1/4	teaspoon salt
1/4	teaspoon pepper
3/4	cup frozen Florida orange juice concentrate, thawed
1/4	cup cold water
2	tablespoons dry sherry
2	teaspoons cornstarch
2	Florida grapefruit, peeled, sectioned and seeded
1	Florida orange, peeled, sectioned and seeded
1	8-ounce can pineapple tidbits, drained
	Fresh chives or sliced green onions
4	cups hot cooked rice, wild rice pilaf or couscous

Season chicken with salt and pepper. Place in a 9x13" baking dish and bake for 25 minutes at 350°. Meanwhile, mix together the orange juice, water, sherry and cornstarch in a medium saucepan. Heat until thickened. Continue heating for 2 more minutes and then add grapefruit and orange sections and pineapple.

When chicken has finished baking, remove from oven and spoon off fat and juice. Pour sauce over chicken and bake for an additional 10 minutes or until chicken is done. Garnish with chives or green onions and serve with rice or couscous.

WILD RICE AND CHICKEN

1	package wild rice
1/3	cup chopped onion
1/4	cup butter
1/4	cup flour
1	teaspoon salt
	Dash of black pepper
1	cup evaporated skim milk
1	cup chicken broth
2	cups chicken, cooked and cubed
1/3	cup chopped pimento
1/3	cup fresh parsley, minced
3	tablespoons blanched almonds, chopped

Preheat oven to 425°. Cook wild rice according to package directions; set aside. Saute onions in butter, blend in flour, salt and pepper. Gradually stir in milk and broth; cook, stirring until thickened. Remove from heat; fold in chicken, pimento, parsley, almonds and cooked rice. Put in 2-quart casserole. Bake for 30 minutes. Easy to do ahead and freeze.

Joanne Durst

HEAVENLY BREAST OF CHICKEN

6	chicken breasts, boned
6	slices bacon
1	package dried beef
	Pepper
2	cans cream of chicken soup
1 1/2	cups sour cream
1	8-ounce package cream cheese

Pepper, but do not salt, chicken breasts. Wrap slice of bacon around edge. Place layer of dried chipped beef in bottom of baking dish. Place chicken on top. Cover with mixture of chicken soup, sour cream and cream cheese; cover. Place in 325° oven for 2 hours. When tender, uncover and let brown. Serve with rice or fine noodles.

Janet Tenney

MATTHEW'S FAVORITE
HONEY-PECAN CHICKEN BREASTS

8	6-ounce chicken breast fillets
1/4	teaspoon salt
1/4	teaspoon pepper
1/4	cup honey
2	tablespoons Dijon mustard
3/4	teaspoon paprika
1/8	teaspoon garlic powder
1 1/4	cups finely crushed corn flakes (about
	4 cups uncrushed cereal)
1/2	cup pecans, finely chopped
	Cooking spray

Preheat oven to 400°. Season chicken with salt and pepper to taste. Combine honey, mustard, paprika and garlic; mix well. Brush both sides of fillets and roll in corn flake and nut mixture. Place chicken on a lightly sprayed cookie sheet. Also lightly spray chicken. Bake at 400° for 20 to 40 minutes or until done, depending on thickness of fillets.

Susan Wener

SAM'S SESAME-GINGER CHICKEN

1	tablespoon sesame seeds, toasted
2	teaspoons grated ginger
2	tablespoons honey
2	tablespoons reduced-sodium soy sauce
4	4-ounce skinned, boned chicken breast halves
	Vegetable cooking spray
	Thin green onion strips (optional)

Stir together sesame seeds, ginger, honey and soy sauce in a small bowl; set aside. Sandwich each chicken breast in between 2 sheets of heavy plastic wrap. Using a rolling pin or meat mallet, flatten to 1/4" thickness. Spray grill rack with vegetable spray and heat over medium-hot coals. Add chicken to rack and cook 4 minutes per side, basting often with soy sauce mixture. Garnish with green onion strips and serve warm. Yields 4 servings.

Liz Fowler

CHICKEN MARINATION

1/2	cup oil
1/2	cup lemon juice
1/4	cup water
2	teaspoons salt
1/4	teaspoon pepper
1	tablespoon sugar
1	teaspoon paprika
1	tablespoon minced onion
1/2	teaspoon garlic salt
	Chicken pieces

Mix first 9 ingredients into a marinade. Put cleaned chicken pieces in a deep pan so each piece is covered with the marinade. Soak overnight and broil the next day.

Jean Dutton

CHICKEN RISSOTO

4 to 5	pounds chicken pieces
1	medium onion, chopped
1 to 2	garlic cloves
1/2	cup oil
1/2	cup mushrooms
1/2	cup dry white wine
1	10-ounce package yellow rice
1	quart chicken broth

Fry chicken, onion and garlic in oil until light brown. Add the mushrooms, wine, rice and chicken broth and cook until rice is done (about 30 minutes). Add water as needed.

Eunice Furtado

CHICKEN IN ORANGE BREAD SAUCE

1	pound white bread, crusts removed
6	ounces Parmesan cheese
1	medium onion
4	ounces butter
1	teaspoon salt
1	chopped clove garlic
	Julienne strips of orange peel
	Slices of 1 red pepper
3	ounces toasted almonds
1	quart milk
	Juice of 5 oranges
8	drops Tabasco
4	teaspoons oregano
4	ounces chicken stock
4	cups cooked rice
	Slices of 1 green pepper
2 1/2	pounds cooked chicken chunks
12	orange sections

Combine bread with milk, Parmesan cheese and orange juice. Saute chopped onion in 2 ounces butter and Tabasco sauce. When onion is transparent, add milk and bread mixture. Place on low fire and cook until ingredients are well blended.

Place oregano and salt in a saucepan and cover with chicken stock. Bring to boil and let simmer until liquid is well flavored. Strain through a fine sieve into milk and bread mixture. Simmer for a few minutes and remove from fire. Smooth in blender. Keep warm.

Saute 1 chopped clove of garlic in 2 ounces butter and add cooked rice. When hot, add julienne strips of orange peel and red and green pepper; mix well. Add cooked chicken chunks to orange sauce; heat.

To serve, make a ring of rice and fill with chicken sauce. Garnish with toasted almonds and orange sections.

NOTE: May be a little complicated, but worth the effort.

Mrs. William LaMothe

CHICKEN MARENGO

4	tablespoons cooking oil
1	4-pound chicken, cut in pieces
	Salt, pepper and flour
1	chopped onion
1	clove garlic
1/4	cup dry white wine
1/2	cup stewed tomatoes or chopped fresh
8	mushrooms

Preheat oven to 375°. Sprinkle chicken pieces with salt, pepper and flour. Brown in cooking oil. Take chicken out and set aside. Then cook in the pan juices, 1 chopped onion and garlic. Add to this, the chicken pieces and 1/4 cup dry white wine, 1/2 cup stewed or chopped fresh tomatoes and mushrooms. Cover and cook slowly until tender (40 to 60 minutes). Makes 6 servings.

Priscilla Fenton

MADISON'S GRANDMOM'S
SUNDAY NIGHT MEAT LOAF

1	pound ground beef
1	can Campbell's chicken and rice soup
1	package dry Lipton onion soup mix
3 to 4	slices American cheese

Mix together everything but cheese and press into loaf pan. Top with cheese slices. Bake at 350° for 1 hour or until done. Serve with mashed potatoes, canned corn and lots of ketchup!

NOTE: An interesting variation that guarantees leftovers for sandwiches: Add 1/2 pound each of ground veal and pork and double the soup quantities.

Karen Hall

Quotable Kid:

I thought it was going to be gross,
but it turned out to be good.
Cody, 5

BOBBIE'S TV MEAT LOAF

1 1/2	pounds lean ground beef
1/2	pound ground pork or lamb
1/2	cup sour cream
1/2	cup chili sauce
2	eggs
1/2	cup bread crumbs, or leftover cooked rice
	Salt and pepper
2	tablespoons chopped fresh dill
2	medium cloves garlic, chopped fine
1	tablespoon butter
2	slices boiled ham
2	large chicken livers
	Parsley for garnish

Preheat oven to 350°. In a large bowl, mix the meats, sour cream, chili sauce, eggs, bread crumbs, salt and pepper, plus the dill and garlic; set aside.

In a saute pan, melt the butter and cook the chicken livers about 3 minutes.

Place half of the meat mixture in a loaf pan. Then take the ham slices and wrap them around the chicken livers. Set them in a row down the middle of the meat. Cover with the rest of the meat and press down so that the ham-liver roll is completely encased. Bake for 1 hour. Cook 10 minutes longer to remove all pink from meat, if desired. Remove from oven and cool for 10 minutes. Remove from pan and garnish with parsley.

When sliced, the layered appearance is pleasing and the ham and livers give an extra bit of taste to an ordinary dish. May be served with a sour cream sauce, prepared by mixing 1 cup sour cream with 1/4 cup chopped fresh dill.

Bobbie Sharp

BETTER BURGERS

2	teaspoons olive oil
4	medium onions, sliced
2	teaspoons sugar
1/4	cup water
2	teaspoons balsamic vinegar
3/4	teaspoon salt, divided
1	pound extra-lean ground beef
2	tablespoons tomato paste
1/4	cup chopped fresh parsley
1/4	teaspoon freshly ground pepper
4	hamburger buns, toasted
4	tomato slices

Warm oil in a large, nonstick skillet. Add onion and sugar; cook over low heat, stirring frequently, until onion is caramel colored (about 20 to 25 minutes). Add water, vinegar and 1/4 teaspoon salt; stir. Place mixture aside, keeping warm.

Mix together ground beef, tomato paste, parsley, remaining salt and pepper; form into 4 patties. Grill over medium-high heat with grill lid closed until desired state of doneness. Serve on buns with caramelized onion and tomato slices. Yields 4 servings.

PICADILLY POCKETS

1	pound ground beef
1	medium onion, chopped
1	clove garlic
2	tablespoons olive oil
2	medium tomatoes, or 1 can, chopped
1/2	cup raisins
1/4	cup slivered almonds
1	teaspoon salt
1	tablespoon vinegar
1/2	teaspoon cinnamon
1/8	teaspoon black pepper
1/4	cup brown sugar
6	pita rounds

Brown meat; drain. Add all other ingredients and simmer gently over low heat for about 20 minutes. Serve in pitas.

Kitchen Tid-Bit:

Adding salt to a sauce is easy; getting rid of too much is a bit tricky. You can do it, however, by dipping a sugar cube in the too-salty sauce and zig-zagging it back and forth over the surface of the sauce three or four times. Taste and repeat if necessary.

MEATY THREE-BEAN CASSEROLE

1/2	pound hamburger
1/2	pound pork sausage
1	cup onion, chopped
1/2	cup ketchup
3/4	cup brown sugar
2	tablespoons vinegar
1	teaspoon dry mustard
1/2	teaspoon salt
1	28-ounce can pork and beans
1	28-ounce can kidney beans
1	28-ounce can butter beans (or limas)

Brown hamburger, sausage and onion. Drain and add remaining ingredients. Bake at 350° for 40 to 45 minutes.

Karen Halverson

SWEDISH MEATBALLS

1 1/2	pounds round steak, ground twice
1/2	pint heavy cream
2	eggs
1	cup soda cracker crumbs (26 crackers)
1	teaspoon sugar
	Salt and pepper

Mix and form balls. Bake at 300° for 1 hour.

Helen Webb

KEY WEST "ROPA VIEJA"
(OLD CLOTHES)

2	pounds flank steak
3	onions
3	green peppers
6	bay leaves
7	cloves garlic
1/4	cup vinegar
1	small can tomato paste
1/4	cup white wine, dry
2	ripe tomatoes
3	tablespoons olive oil
	Salt and pepper to taste
	Dash of Tabasco sauce

Salt steak lightly and place in large skillet or Dutch oven over medium-high heat. Cover with 1 green pepper, chopped, 1 onion, chopped, 3 cloves garlic, chopped fine and 3 bay leaves. Pour over this 1/4 cup of vinegar. Bring to boil. Reduce heat to simmer, cover pan and simmer for 1 to 1 1/2 hours until meat is quite tender. Cool meat, then strip meat into pieces. Fry out remaining chopped onions, pepper and garlic in olive oil. Add meat, 3 bay leaves, 1/4 cup dry white wine and small amount of broth (1/2 to 1 cup) and simmer about 15 minutes. Stir in tomato paste and 2 ripe tomatoes, chopped. Simmer until tomatoes are cooked and paste blended. Serve over white rice and accompany with black beans (frijoles negros). Beans may be topped with chopped raw onion if desired.

Charlotte White

FABULOUS FILLET OF BEEF WITH BEARNAISE
(A REAL HOLIDAY FAVORITE)

1	fillet of beef tenderloin, whole
	Kosher salt
	Dijon mustard
	Fine bread crumbs
	BEARNAISE SAUCE:
6	green onions, chopped
1/4	cup tarragon vinegar
4	egg yolks
2	teaspoons dry tarragon
1/4	teaspoon salt
1/4	teaspoon dry mustard
	Dash of Tabasco
1	cup melted butter

Cut 1" deep gash down the length of the fillet. Rub with kosher salt. Coat with Dijon mustard and roll in fine bread crumbs. Roast at 400° until meat thermometer registers rare. Slice, reassemble and fill gash with Bearnaise Sauce.

SAUCE: Combine vinegar and onions in a skillet; reduce almost completely. Place in a blender with egg yolks, tarragon, salt, mustard and Tabasco. Slowly add hot melted butter and whirl until smooth.

Sharon Chamberlain

SOPHIE'S NANNY'S HOLIDAY BRISKET

1   whole beef brisket, deckle (that's the fatty outside layer) intact

2   envelopes Lipton onion soup mix

Preheat oven to 350°. Find a roasting pan just large enough to hold the brisket. Lay out a big sheet of heavy-duty aluminum foil. Sprinkle it with one package of the soup mix. Put brisket on top of soup mix. Cover top of brisket with the other packet of soup mix. You don't need to add any water. Seal the brisket TIGHTLY in foil. It is imperative that no juices escape during the cooking. When you think you've got it sufficiently wrapped, add another layer of foil!

Slow-roast for 5 to 6 hours. (If desired, during the final 1 1/2 hours of cooking, add to the oven a pan of potatoes, carrots and onions tossed with a bit of olive oil. They will roast beautifully!) Unwrap the cooked brisket and transfer the meat to a platter. It will practically fall apart on its own, but slice it for your guests' convenience!

GRAVY: To the juices remaining in the roasting pan, add 1 can of beef broth, 1 can of water and 3 tablespoons flour, plus salt and pepper to taste. Cook over medium heat until bubbly. Serve over the brisket and roasted veggies.

NOTE: Be prepared for all your guests to demand this recipe. Tell them it is a sacred family secret!

Ariel Mellman

REUBEN CASSEROLE

1 3/4	cups fresh or canned sauerkraut
2	cups (1/2 pound) shredded Swiss cheese
2	medium tomatoes, thinly sliced
1/2	cup (1 stick) butter
1/4	teaspoon caraway seeds
1/2	pound thinly sliced corned beef
3	tablespoons Thousand Island dressing
2	tablespoons butter
1	cup crumbled, seasoned rye wafers

Butter 1 1/2-quart casserole. Drain sauerkraut. Thinly layer sauerkraut in bottom of casserole. Top with sliced corned beef, then shredded cheese. Dribble Thousand Island dressing on top of cheese. Add tomatoes, thinly sliced or 2 cups. Dot with 2 tablespoons butter. Melt butter in small saucepan. Saute crumbled rye wafers, add caraway seeds. Spread on top of other ingredients. Bake for 30 minutes until bubbly at 425°. Makes 4 to 6 servings.

Mrs. Clifford Bartelt

BEANS AND RICE AND SAUSAGE

2   cans black beans
2   cans red kidney beans
1   can drained tomatoes, chopped
2   good sized cloves garlic, minced
4   stalks celery (some leaves), chopped
3   good sized onions, diced
1   good size bay leaf
1   teaspoon thyme (or 1/2 teaspoon oregano)
1   tablespoon parsley (if dried, more if fresh)
1   teaspoon curry (if you like it, I do)
1   good sized ring Italian sausage (or 1/2
       pound ham or 1/2 pound chopped meat)
1   good sized shot sherry or 1 tablespoon
       vinegar
1   sweet carrot, diced
1   good teaspoon chili powder
       Salt and pepper

Use canned beans, it's easier. Use 2 kinds, it's prettier. Start with sausage, brown and toss off fat. Add oil to just sheet the pot; heat. Add onions, garlic; brown lightly. Add chopped celery (some leaves). Add beans, seasonings and vegetables. Add sherry or vinegar. Bring to boil. Turn down to simmer for about 3/4 of an hour. Cut the sausage into chunks, one for each dish. Serve, topped with an ice cream ball of rice in the center of the dish, or let people dish out as much as they want of rice.

Sylvia Mintz

PEPPER-HONEY PORK TENDERLOINS

1	tablespoon grated fresh ginger
1	jalapeno pepper, seeded and finely chopped
1/4	teaspoon dried crushed red pepper
1/3	cup honey
3	tablespoons soy sauce
3	tablespoons sesame oil
2	3/4-pound pork tenderloins
	Garnish (optional): fresh jalapeno peppers

Mix ginger, pepper, honey, soy sauce and sesame oil in a plastic bag and add tenderloins. Seal bag and refrigerate for 8 hours, turning periodically. Discard marinade and place tenderloins on the rack of a broiler pan that has been coated with vegetable cooking spray. Place broiler pan 5" from heat and broil for 5 minutes on each side, or until meat temperature reaches 160°. Slice the tenderloins and garnish with fresh jalapeno peppers. Yields 4 to 6 servings.

RUBBED PORK WITH CORN AND BEAN SALAD

1	10-ounce package frozen corn, cooked and drained
1	15-ounce can black beans, drained and rinsed
1/3	cup green pepper, chopped
1	jar pimento (or roasted red pepper), chopped
1/2	cup green onions, finely chopped
2	tablespoons olive oil
2	tablespoons red wine vinegar
1	tablespoon water
1	teaspoon chili powder
1	teaspoon sugar
1	teaspoon cumin
1/4	teaspoon salt
2	whole pork tenderloins
2	tablespoons garlic salt
1	tablespoon cumin
2	tablespoons Italian seasoning

Cook and drain corn. Drain can of beans, rinse in cold water. Add green pepper, pimento or roasted pepper and green onion. Mix oil, vinegar, water and seasonings in a jar. Shake thoroughly. Add to corn, bean mixture; chill. Can make a day ahead. Mix garlic salt, chili powder, cumin and Italian seasonings together in a small bowl. Trim fat from tenderloins. Rub all over with seasoned mixture. Grill or broil on medium until just done. Can be slightly pink in the center. Mound salad in the center of a large platter. Slice the tenderloin into 1/2" slices and place around the salad. Meat can be served at room temperature. Great for a hot summer evening. Serve with a loaf of fresh French bread.

HONEY PORK

1   2-pound pork tenderloin
1   cup honey
4   tablespoons lemon grass
     (lemon-peppers can be substituted
     if necessary)
2   tablespoons vegetable oil
2   tablespoons fish sauce (Vietnamese or
     Thai are best)
     Handful thinly chopped scallions

Slice the pork tenderloin about 1/4" thick. The size is not important, but the thickness is. Combine honey, lemon grass or lemon-peppers, vegetable oil, fish sauce and half the scallions into a bowl and mix well. Add pork to marinade and mix with hands until meat is well coated. Let sit for at least 30 minutes, the longer the better (overnight is best). Cook meat over the grill until desired degree of doneness. Garnish with remaining chopped scallions. Makes 4 servings.

Thomas Doran,
Lori Gretz

TRUESDALE HAM

3	ham steaks, 1 1/2" thick
3	tablespoons prepared mustard
	Flour as needed
3/4	pound mushrooms, fresh
3	tablespoons brown sugar
1	tablespoon vinegar
1	can stewed tomatoes
1/2	pint light cream

Remove bone pieces from ham and trim off fat. Makes paste of brown sugar, mustard, vinegar and flour. Spread on all sides of ham. Place in baking pan. Pour tomatoes over ham. Bake in SLOW oven (275 to 300°) for 3 hours. Add mushroom stems and caps. Add cream. Bake 1/2 hour more. Slice and serve with rice. Makes 8 to 10 servings.

Ruth Lowry

GLAZED PORK CHOPS

6	thick loin pork chops
1/2	cup unsweetened pineapple juice
2	teaspoons dry mustard
12	whole coriander seeds, crushed
	Lemon slices
2	cups sugar
1/2	cup honey
6	whole cloves
	Orange slices
	Maraschino cherries

Brown chops and season with salt and pepper. Place in shallow baking dish. Combine cloves, pineapple juice, mustard, coriander, sugar, honey and spoon 3 tablespoons over each chop. Bake, uncovered, at 350° for 1 1/2 hours, basting frequently. Place orange and lemon slices and maraschino cherries on chops with toothpicks. Baste again and bake 10 more minutes. Makes 6 servings.

Judy Thompson

VEAL SCALLOPINE

1 1/2	pounds veal, thinly sliced
3/4	cup grated Parmesan cheese (or as an alternative, use flour)
	Salt
	Freshly ground pepper (if flour is used)
3	tablespoons butter
1	cup thinly sliced fresh mushrooms
1/2	cup dry Marsala or any dry white table wine
1/2	cup bouillon
1	tablespoon flour

Sprinkle veal with Parmesan cheese or flour (or combination of both) and pound thin. Saute mushrooms in butter and remove from pan. Brown veal in same pan and remove. Lightly salt meat. Add wine and bouillon to drippings and bring to a boil. Blend 1 tablespoon flour into gravy and simmer to thicken. Return veal and mushrooms to pan and simmer 10 to 15 minutes or until veal is tender. Makes 4 servings.

Betty Niemeier

VEAL PARMESAN

1/4	cup fine bread crumbs
1/2	teaspoon salt
	Dash of pepper
1	beaten egg
2	tablespoons olive oil or salad oil
2	8-ounce cans tomato sauce
2	teaspoons crushed oregano
1/4	cup grated Parmesan cheese
1/2	teaspoon paprika
5	veal cutlets or loin chops, 3/4" thick
1	tablespoon water
5	thin slices mozzarella cheese
2	cloves garlic, crushed

Mix crumbs, Parmesan cheese, salt, paprika and pepper. Dip chops in egg that has been beaten with 1 tablespoon water, then in crumb mixture. Brown on both sides in hot oil. Place a slice of mozzarella cheese on top of each chop. Mix tomato sauce and garlic, pour over chops; sprinkle with oregano. Cover; simmer 50 minutes or until meat is done. Makes 5 servings.

Mrs. Leland Moree, Jr.

Notes

CATCH OF THE DAY

Fabulous Ways to Fix Fish

SHRIMP AND CORN CAKES

1	12-ounce package Stouffer's corn souffle
3	cups finely chopped cooked shrimp
1	4 1/2-ounce can chopped green chilies
1	4-ounce jar pimento
7	green onions, chopped
1 1/2	teaspoons chili powder
1/2	teaspoon cumin
1/8	teaspoon salt
1/8	teaspoon pepper
2	cups fine, dry bread crumbs, divided
1/4	cup vegetable oil

Thaw corn souffle in microwave at medium for 6 to 7 minutes. Combine corn souffle and next 8 ingredients in a large bowl; stir in 1/2 cup bread crumbs. Cover and chill 1 hour or overnight. Shape corn mixture into 10 patties and coat with remaining 1 1/2 cups bread crumbs. Cook half of corn cakes in 2 tablespoons of hot oil in a large skillet over medium-high heat for 3 to 4 minutes on each side or until cakes are golden brown. Drain on paper towels. Repeat procedure with remaining oil and cakes. Serve with guacamole and black bean salsa.

Cindy Sitton

CURRIED SHRIMP WITH RICE

2	medium onions
2	cloves garlic, chopped
1/4	pound butter or margarine
4	tablespoons flour
1	cup chicken stock
1	cup heavy cream or Coffee Rich
1	teaspoon salt
1	tablespoon curry powder (you can use up to 2 tablespoons at your own peril!)
1	teaspoon ginger
	Dash red pepper
1	cup rice, cooked
1	pound freshly cooked shrimp

Cook onions and garlic in butter or margarine. Add flour and put in top of double boiler. (This can be done in the morning.) Then add 1 cup chicken stock, 1 cup heavy cream, salt, curry, ginger and red pepper. Cook until thick. Add rice and cooked shrimp.

NOTE: This is from Connie Stackpole, who had a home ec radio program in N.H., called THE RED BARN, where she served this delectable dish with roast beef every Sunday by reservation only. We have enjoyed it for years.

Juliet Miller

SHRIMP SANTIVA

1 1/2	pounds shrimp
1 1/2	cup hot cream
1/4	cup butter
	Salt
1	clove garlic, mashed
1	cup toasted bread crumbs
3/4	cup chopped parsley
4	tablespoons grated Parmesan cheese
	Pepper

Pour hot cream over crumbs, mix well; let stand. Add parsley, garlic and butter. Spread 1/2 bread crumb mix in flat baking dish. Add 1 layer shrimp, then 1 layer bread mix, then layer shrimp. Sprinkle with cheese. Bake 1/2 hour at 350°. Makes 4 servings.

Cynthia Conant

THAI SHRIMP DISH

This is an easy and delightful dish from Thailand that permits one to utilize some of the best food products on the islands. It should be served at room temperature (assuming your room isn't too hot!). For added spice, garnish it with a couple of teaspoons of crushed dried red chili peppers.

2	pounds large shrimp
2	sweet peppers, green or red
2	mangos
	Lemon juice
2	tablespoons peanut oil
2	medium cloves garlic, minced
2	tablespoons shallots or scallions, minced
1/2	teaspoon anchovy paste
1	tablespoon light soy sauce
2	tablespoons crushed roasted peanuts, unsalted
1 to 2	cups coconut cream*

Broil the shrimp, unshelled, for about 4 minutes on each side. Shell and devein and quarter them lengthwise. Place the whole peppers on a fork over a flame, turning slowly until the skin is charred. Then peel and slice them into strips about the size of the quartered shrimp. Peel mangos and cut into similar strips. Sprinkle with lemon juice. Combine shrimp, peppers and mangos. Saute the garlic and shallots or scallions in hot oil until golden. Add, along with pan drippings, to the shrimp mixture. Blend the anchovy paste and soy sauce; add to the mixture. Toss gently. Sprinkle with peanuts, then gradually add sufficient coconut cream to coat all the ingredients. Season to taste, adding more soy sauce/anchovy paste mixture if desired. Makes 6 to 8 servings.

* To make coconut cream, cover the grated meat of 2 fresh coconuts with 2 cups scalded milk and steep for 20 minutes. Strain through a fine sieve lined with double cheesecloth, pressing firmly to extract all of the liquid. This will make about 2 cups.

Don and Grace Whitehead

SHRIMP HARPIN
(SHRIMP AND RICE CASSEROLE)

2 1/2	pounds fresh shrimp
1	tablespoon lemon juice
3	tablespoons salad oil
3/4	cup cooked rice
1/2	cup minced green pepper
1/4	cup minced onion
1	teaspoon salt
1/8	teaspoon mace
	Dash of cayenne pepper
1	can tomato soup
1/2	cup sherry
3/4	cup blanched almonds

Preheat oven to 350°. Cook shrimp in boiling salted water for 5 minutes; drain. Set aside 8 shrimp for garnish. Place shrimp in a 2-quart casserole. Sprinkle with lemon juice and salad oil. Saute green pepper and onion in butter for 5 minutes. Add all ingredients to shrimp and mix well. Bake, uncovered, for 35 minutes. Then top with 8 shrimp and almonds. Bake 20 minutes longer or until mixture is bubbly.

Bella Kontinos

SHRIMP SCAMPI

2	pounds large raw shrimp
1/2	cup butter or margarine
1	teaspoon salt
6	cloves garlic, crushed
1/4	cup chopped parsley
2	teaspoons grated lemon peel
2	tablespoons lemon juice
6	lemon wedges

Preheat oven to 400°. Remove shells from shrimp, leaving shell on tail section only. Devein, wash under running water and drain on paper towels. Melt butter in baking pan in oven. Add salt, garlic and 1 tablespoon parsley; mix well. Arrange shrimp in single layer in baking dish. Bake, uncovered, 5 minutes. Turn shrimp, sprinkle with lemon peel, lemon juice and remaining parsley. Bake 8 to 10 minutes or just until tender. Arrange shrimp on heated serving platter. Pour garlic butter over all. Garnish with lemon wedges.

Bella Kontinos

EXCELLENT AND EASY SHRIMP CASSEROLE

2	cans cream of shrimp soup
1 1/3	cups milk
1	cup mayonnaise
3	cups fine noodles, not cooked
1	pound shrimp
1/2	cup Cheddar cheese, grated
1	can fried onion rings

Preheat oven to 350°. Combine the first 5 ingredients and pour into a 9x12" casserole dish. Top with the Cheddar cheese; bake, covered, for 30 minutes. Uncover and sprinkle with the fried onion rings. Bake an additional 10 minutes, uncovered. Serves 6 to 8.

Mary Beth Greenplate

J.D.'S MOM'S SHRIMP CAKES

1/2	pound fresh asparagus, blanched and chopped
4	tablespoons butter
2/3	cup plus 3 tablespoons chopped shallots
1 1/2	pounds uncooked shrimp (16 to 20 count), chopped
1/2	pound uncooked sea scallops, chopped
1 1/2	cups bread crumbs
1	cup diced red pepper
2	large eggs, beaten
1/4	cup chopped scallions

Mix everything except butter and form into cakes. This can be done a couple of hours ahead. Melt 1 to 2 tablespoons butter over medium-high heat and cook cakes 5 minutes per side. Repeat with remaining cakes.

Karen Hall

SPICY ROASTED SHRIMP

Serve them on their own as a first course, or if you're hungry, add rice, beans and guacamole.

24   jumbo shrimp, in the shell, butterflied

MARINADE:
2   tablespoons fresh lime juice
3   tablespoons olive oil
1/2   teaspoon seeded, deribbed and chopped jalapenos
1   clove garlic, smashed, peeled and chopped fine
        Kosher salt to taste
        Freshly ground black pepper to taste

Place shrimp, shell side down, in an 18x13x2" roasting pan. Whisk together marinade and pour over shrimp. Set aside for 1 hour, turning over once. Before roasting, place rack in the center of the oven and preheat to 500°. Roast shrimp, flesh side down, in the pan for 2 1/2 minutes. Turn shrimp over and roast 2 1/2 minutes more. Pour pan juices over shrimp and serve warm or at room temperature. Serves 3.

CONNOR'S SHRIMP AND CARAMELIZED ONION QUESADILLA

2   tablespoons butter or olive oil
1   large vidalia or red onion, sliced
1   tablespoon butter or olive oil
1   pound (16 to 20 count) shrimp
1   package shredded cheese (Cheddar,
      Monterey Jack or mixture)
    Medium size tortilla shells
    Homemade or store bought salsa
    Sour cream

Over medium-high heat, melt 2 tablespoons butter and saute sliced onion until caramelized to a soft brown color. This will take about 20 minutes, stirring occasionally; set aside. Devein shrimp and saute in 1 tablespoon butter until just pink. Remove from pan and slice each shrimp in half lengthwise.

TO ASSEMBLE: On tortilla, place some cheese, shrimp and onions. Top with more cheese and cover with second tortilla. Place on cookie sheet. Heat in 350° oven until cheese melts. Serve with salsa and sour cream.

NOTE: This can be made a few hours ahead and refrigerated until ready to heat.

Karen Hall

SAUTEED SHRIMP WITH PESTO

1 1/2	pounds large uncooked shrimp
1	cup basil leaves, packed
1/2	cup Italian parsley
2	cloves garlic, peeled
3	tablespoons grated Parmesan cheese
1	teaspoon salt
1/2	teaspoon fresh pepper
2	tablespoons olive oil
1	cup low-sodium chicken broth
2	tablespoons fresh lemon juice
4	cups cooked basmati rice

Peel and devein the shrimp; rinse and refrigerate. Combine the basil, parsley, garlic, Parmesan cheese, half the salt and half the pepper in a blender or food processor. Process for 30 seconds. Add 1 tablespoon of the olive oil and 3/4 cup of the chicken broth through the top of the blender or food processor while the machine is running. Process into a paste; set aside.

In a large nonstick skillet over medium-high heat, heat the remaining olive oil and 1/4 cup chicken broth for 1 minute. Add shrimp and saute until pink (3 to 4 minutes). Season with lemon juice and remaining salt and pepper. Serve the shrimp and pesto over rice. Garnish with steamed vegetables. Serves 4.

BIG RUDY'S SHRIMP TOAST

1/2	pound fresh or frozen raw shrimp
1/2	cup chopped green onions (with tops)
1/4	cup all-purpose flour
1/4	cup water
1	egg
1	tablespoon cornstarch
1	teaspoon salt
1/4	teaspoon sugar
1/4	teaspoon sesame oil
	Dash of white pepper
	Vegetable oil
5	slices white bread

Peel and devein shrimp. Cut lengthwise into halves and crosswise into halves. Mix shrimp, green onions, flour, water, egg, cornstarch, salt, sugar, sesame oil and white pepper. Heat vegetable oil (1 1/2" deep) in wok to 350°. Remove crusts from bread and cut each slice into 4 squares. Place 1 or 2 pieces of shrimp with the sauce on each square. Fry 4 or 5 squares at a time until golden brown, turning frequently (about 2 minutes). Drain on paper towels. Makes 20 appetizers.

TIP: Refrigerate prepared Shrimp Toast up to 24 hours. Before serving, heat, uncovered, in a 400° oven until hot (12 to 15 minutes). Drain on paper towels.

Sandy Zahorchak

PASTA FAGIOLI WITH SHRIMP

1	tablespoon olive oil
1	cup chopped bacon
1	small Spanish onion, chopped
5	garlic cloves, finely chopped
1	celery stalk, chopped
1 1/2	tablespoons chopped fresh rosemary leaves
3	cups cooked navy or pinto beans, rinsed
2 to 3	cups chicken broth
3/4	pound spaghetti or fettuccine

SHRIMP:

1	tablespoon olive oil
1 1/4	pounds large (about 20) shrimp, peeled and deveined
1/2	teaspoon kosher salt
1/2	teaspoon black pepper
2	garlic cloves, thinly sliced
1/2	cup dry white wine
1/4	cup chopped fresh flat-leaf parsley leaves
2	tablespoons chopped scallion greens
1/4 to 1/2	teaspoon unsalted butter, Fresh rosemary sprigs, for garnish

In a large saucepan, over low heat, add 1 tablespoon oil and the bacon; cook 2 minutes. Add the onions, garlic, celery and rosemary, stirring well after each addition. Cook until the onion is soft, about 4 to 5 minutes. Turn heat to medium and add the beans and 2 cups chicken broth. Simmer adding more broth if necessary, until the beans begin to break apart, about 30 minutes.

Pour the bean mixture into a food processor or blender; puree. For a creamier, richer puree, gradually add up to 1/2 cup olive oil (optional); set aside.

Cook pasta as directed. Drain pasta, reserving 1 cup of the pasta water. While the pasta is cooking, start the shrimp by seasoning with salt and pepper. Add the oil to a large skillet, heated over medium heat. Add the shrimp and cook until the shrimp is pink and opaque, about 3 minutes. Add the wine and cook until slightly reduced, about 2 minutes. Fold in the bean puree, adding some of the pasta water if the sauce is too thick. Add the pasta and cook until heated through. Add the parsley, scallion greens, cheese, red pepper flakes and the butter, stirring well after each addition. Divide into broad flat bowls, garnished with fresh rosemary sprigs. Serves 4 to 6.

Kevin Pierce

SHRIMP AND ARTICHOKE CASSEROLE

7	tablespoons butter
1	cup mushrooms, chopped
4	tablespoons flour
3/4	cup milk
3/4	cup heavy cream
1/4	cup sherry
1	tablespoon Worcestershire sauce
1/2	cup sliced water chestnuts
	Salt and fresh ground pepper to taste
1	can artichoke hearts, drained
1	pound (16 to 20 count) shrimp, cooked and cleaned
1/4	cup Parmesan cheese
	Paprika for garnish

Preheat oven to 375°. In skillet over medium heat, melt butter and saute chopped mushrooms for 2 minutes. Stir in flour and blend. Gradually whisk in milk and cream, stirring constantly. Add the sherry, Worcestershire sauce and water chestnuts. Season with salt and pepper; taste. You might want to add more sherry. Remove from stove; set aside.

In a 2-quart casserole with a lid, arrange the artichokes on the bottom and top with shrimp. Gently pour the sauce over the shrimp and artichokes. Top with Parmesan and sprinkle with paprika. Cover and bake for 30 to 35 minutes. Serve on a bed of rice. Serves 6 (leftovers freeze beautifully).

Bobbie Sharp

HONEY SESAME SHRIMP ON THE GRILL

1 1/2	pounds jumbo shrimp
2	green onions
2	garlic cloves, crushed with garlic press
2	slices (1/4" thick) peeled fresh ginger
3	tablespoons dry sherry
3	tablespoons soy sauce
1 1/2	tablespoons honey
1 1/2	tablespoons sesame seeds
1	tablespoon Thai sweet chili sauce (optional)
1/2	teaspoon Chinese five-spice powder
5	tablespoons Asian sesame oil

Shell and devein shrimp, leaving on tail part of shell if you like. Rinse with cold water. Dry with paper towel; set aside. Trim green onions. Crush white part of green onions with side of chef's knife. Thinly slice green parts and reserve for garnish. In large bowl, combine white part of green onions, garlic, ginger, sherry, soy sauce, honey, sesame seeds, Thai chili sauce (if using), five-spice powder and 3 tablespoons sesame oil. Stir in shrimp and refrigerate, covered, 30 minutes to 1 hour. Transfer shrimp from marinade to another bowl. Pour marinade into small saucepan; discard ginger and white part of green onions. Cook marinade over medium-high heat until thick and syrupy, about 2 minutes; set aside. Toss or brush shrimp with remaining 2 tablespoons sesame oil. Place shrimp on grill over high heat and cook 8 to 10 minutes, until shrimp turn opaque throughout, turning once and brushing with reduced marinade during last 2 minutes of cooking. Transfer shrimp to platter and garnish with sliced green onions. Makes 4 main dish servings.

SHRIMP IN TOMATO SAUCE
WITH FETA CHEESE

1 1/2	pounds medium shrimp, shelled and deveined
1/2	cup chopped onion
2	tablespoons olive oil
1	clove garlic, minced fine
1	15-ounce can tomato sauce
1/4	cup dry white wine
1/4	cup fresh parsley, chopped
1/4	teaspoon cayenne pepper or red pepper flakes
	Salt and pepper to taste
6	ounces crumbled feta cheese

Saute onion in olive oil until transparent. Add garlic, tomato sauce, wine, parsley and red pepper. Simmer, uncovered, 20 minutes, stirring often. Add shrimp to sauce and cook 5 minutes. Spray a casserole dish with cooking spray. Layer crumbled feta cheese over the bottom of the dish. Pour shrimp and sauce over cheese. Bake for 10 minutes at 450°. Serve over rice. Garnish with chopped parsley.

Cindy Sitton

SCALLOPED OYSTERS

1	pint oysters
2	cups medium to coarse saltine cracker crumbs
1/2	cup butter
	Fresh ground pepper to taste
3/4	cup light cream
1/4	cup oyster liquid
1/4	teaspoon Worcestershire sauce
1/2	teaspoon salt

Preheat oven to 350°. Drain oysters and save 1/4 cup liquid. Melt butter in skillet and add cracker crumbs. Stir for 2 to 3 minutes to toast slightly. In a small, greased casserole or souffle dish, spread one-third of the crumbs. Cover with half of the oysters. Sprinkle with pepper. Spread another third of the crumbs over oysters. Cover with remaining oysters. Sprinkle with pepper. Combine cream, oyster liquid, Worcestershire sauce and salt. Pour over oysters. Top with remaining cracker crumbs. Bake for 40 minutes.

Cindy Pierce

DEVILED OYSTERS

1	pint oysters with liquid
1	cup cracker crumbs
1/4	cup parsley, chopped fine
2	teaspoons Worcestershire sauce
2	hard-boiled eggs, chopped
1/2	cup light cream
	Cayenne pepper to taste
1/4	cup melted butter or margarine
1	medium green pepper, chopped fine
1	medium onion, grated
1/4	teaspoon dry mustard
3	eggs, lightly beaten
	Salt to taste

Combine all ingredients in buttered 6-cup casserole. Bake at 375° for 30 minutes or until set and lightly browned. For individual servings, bake in ramekins or scallop shells for 15 minutes. For hors d'oeuvres, bake in oyster or clam shells for 10 minutes.

Evelyn Piggot

ELLIE'S OSCAR DE LASAGNA

8	lasagna noodles, cooked
16	spears fresh asparagus, lightly steamed and halved
2	cups crab meat (stone crab in season or king crab)
1/2	cup chopped celery
2	tablespoons chopped onion
2	tablespoons butter
1/2	cup Italian bread crumbs
1/4	cup mayonnaise
1	egg
1/2	teaspoon salt
1/2	teaspoon paprika

Saute the celery and onion in the 2 tablespoons butter until soft. Combine with other filling ingredients (except asparagus) in a large bowl; mix well. Divide filling mixture evenly between the lasagna noodles and roll up with asparagus in the middle. Place in a greased baking dish, cover and bake in a 350° oven for 25 minutes. Serve warm topped with Hollandaise Sauce. Serves 4.

HOLLANDAISE SAUCE:

3	eggs
4	teaspoons lemon juice
3	tablespoons water
7	tablespoons butter
2	dashes hot sauce

Combine eggs, lemon juice and water in a small bowl. Whisk until blended. In a heavy non-stick skillet, melt the butter with the hot sauce. Add egg mixture slowly, stirring constantly until thick. Do not overcook. Add 1/2 teaspoon salt before serving.

Captain Randy Barfield

FISH WITH DILL

2	pounds white fish (grouper is great)
1	cup plain yogurt
1/2	cup mayonnaise
1	tablespoon white wine
1	tablespoon lemon juice
2	teaspoons dill weed
	Curry powder, 2 shakes of can

Place the fish in a flat baking dish. Pour over the top of fish the other combined ingredients. Bake, uncovered, in 350° oven for 30 to 35 minutes. Makes 4 servings.

Mary Lee

ANY CATCH WILL DO

1   8-ounce fish fillet per serving (trout,
       grouper, redfish, snook)
1   egg
1   tablespoon hot sauce
1/2   cup flour
1/2   cup cornmeal
1/4   cup Italian bread crumbs
    Vegetable oil

In a medium bowl, beat egg and hot sauce; set aside. In a larger bowl, mix together the flour, cornmeal and bread crumbs; set aside. Pour enough oil into a heavy skillet to cover the bottom. Dip fillets, one at a time, in the egg mixture, roll in the cornmeal mixture and saute in the oil until browned on both sides. Serve with tartar or cocktail sauce.

TARTAR SAUCE:

1/2   cup mayonnaise
1   tablespoon grated onion
1   tablespoon grated sweet pickle
1   tablespoon spicy mustard
    Salt and pepper to taste

Mix and serve.

Captain Randy Barfield

SMOKED FISH

Fish fillets
Vinegar in cayenne pepper
Salt

Anyone can smoke fish. It only takes a desire, time to do it and space out of doors to set up equipment. An enclosure may be made with used lumber, with wire shelves from a discarded refrigerator or freezer. Place fish fillets on shelves. Season by sprinkling lightly with salt and vinegar from a jar of cayenne peppers. Build a low fire under the fish, using buttonwood. The temperature inside the enclosure should be kept at 140° for 5 to 5 1/2 hours. The fish is then cooked and ready to eat, or can be frozen and kept up until wanted.

NOTE: A discarded refrigerator may be used for a fish smoker if ventilated and a damper fixed to control the amount of fire.

"Uncle Joe" Wightman

FISH IN COCONUT MILK

4   fillets of fish
Freshly ground black pepper
2   cups milk
3   large tomatoes, sliced thin
Salt
1   cup fresh grated coconut
2   large onions, cut in rings

Wash and dry the fish. Sprinkle with salt and pepper on both sides and arrange in a single layer in a buttered casserole. Refrigerate until ready to bake.

Rinse the coconut under cold running water, then combine in a saucepan with the milk. Bring to a boil, remove from heat and let stand at room temperature for 30 minutes. Run the mixture in a blender or strain pressing out all the liquid.

Spread the onions over the fish, then cover with tomatoes. Pour the coconut milk over all. Bake in preheated oven, 375° for 45 minutes. Serve directly from the casserole.

NOTE: Do not use "sugar added" coconut.

Jean Bair

SUNSHINE CITRUS FISH

5 or 6	fillets of fresh red snapper, grouper or pompano (about 2 pounds)
12	orange sections (more or less)
12	grapefruit sections (more or less)
2	cups mayonnaise
1/2	cup orange or grapefruit juice
	Dash paprika or nutmeg
	Parsley for garnish

Line shallow baking dish or jellyroll pan with foil. Arrange fish fillets on foil, skin side down (if there is skin). Sprinkle fish with salt and pepper. Frost fillets with mayonnaise and orange juice mixture. Arrange grapefruit and orange sections and then finish with remaining mayonnaise mixture. Sprinkle with paprika or nutmeg. Bake at 350° until fish flakes when forked (8 to 12 minutes, depending on thickness). Garnish with parsley and serve immediately. Makes 6 servings.

Shirley Evans

BAKED FISH WITH SHRIMP SAUCE

1 1/2	pounds fish fillets
1	cup milk
	Dash of pepper
2	tablespoons flour
1/4	cup grated processed American cheese
1	pound fresh shrimp
1	teaspoon salt
2	tablespoons butter
2	tablespoons sherry

Dice shrimp after cooking, cleaning and shelling. Wipe fillets dry with paper towels and place in shallow baking dish with milk, salt and pepper. Bake at 350° for 30 minutes. Meanwhile, melt butter in double boiler and stir in flour. When fish is done, pour off milk from fish and add to butter and flour. Cook sauce, stirring constantly, until thickened. Add shrimp, sherry and cheese. Pour over fish. Broil until lightly browned. Makes 4 servings.

Fran Scholefield

BAKED FILLETS IN SOUR CREAM

Lime juice
Fish
Onion
Sour cream
Margarine
Salt
Paprika

Heat oven to 400°. Cover bottom of shallow baking dish with margarine. Use a liberal amount of lime juice to coat dish; salt and place fish in baking dish. Cover each fillet with slices of onion. Cover and bake for 20 minutes. Uncover, pour over sour cream, sprinkle with paprika. Place in low broiler until cream is lightly browned. Serve with a baked potato and salad. Fish fillets are good also in a sauce made with 1 or 2 cans of tomato sauce, olive oil, a little garlic or onion and oregano. Spoon sauce over fish several times while simmering. Heat sauce to boiling before adding fish. Serve over rice.

BROILED SALMON WITH SPRING SALAD

6	4-ounce salmon fillets

SALAD:

1	small head Boston lettuce
1	small head oakleaf or red leaf lettuce
1	small head radicchio
1	small head Belgian endive
12	leaves fresh spinach
1	pablano chili or bell pepper, julienned

VINAIGRETTE:

1/2	cup Wisconsin Pepato or asiago cheese, grated
1	tablespoon fresh basil, chopped
1	tablespoon fresh chives, chopped
1/4	cup sherry vinegar or white wine vinegar
3/4	cup extra virgin olive oil
1	clove garlic, crushed

SALAD: Prepare spring salad greens, using 2 pieces of each green per serving; refrigerate.

VINAIGRETTE: Prepare vinaigrette by mixing all ingredients; set aside.

Preheat broiler. Brush salmon fillets with olive oil; season with salt and pepper. Broil fillets 3 to 5 minutes per side until just opaque in the center.

Toss salad with vinaigrette. Arrange on each dinner plate, topping each salad with a salmon fillet. Serves 6.

Nancy Gerhard

SALMON WITH BALSAMIC CITRUS GLAZE

4	6-ounce salmon fillets
1/4	cup fresh-squeezed grapefruit juice
2	ounces maple syrup
2	cups balsamic vinegar
1/4	cup frozen orange juice concentrate, thawed
1	cup fresh diced oranges
1	cup fresh diced grapefruit
2	tablespoons fresh chopped tarragon
1	pound asparagus
1	cup fresh squeezed grapefruit juice

Marinate salmon in 1/4 cup grapefruit juice and maple syrup for 30 minutes.

Poach asparagus in 1 cup grapefruit juice for 1 minute; set aside.

In a saute pan, bring balsamic vinegar to a boil and cook on high heat for 10 minutes or until reduced by half. Add orange juice concentrate and cook for 3 more minutes. Remove from heat and add oranges, grapefruit and tarragon; set aside.

In a nonstick grill pan (or grill sprayed with cooking spray) on medium-high heat, place salmon face down and cook for 2 minutes. Rotate fillets 45° and cook (on the same side) for 2 more minutes. Turn over and cook for 3 minutes.

Arrange asparagus on plates, place salmon on top of asparagus and top with the balsamic citrus glaze. Serves 4.

MILE MARKER SNAPPER

2	tomatoes, peeled and thinly sliced
3	tablespoons soft, fresh bread crumbs
	Salt and pepper
1 1/2	pounds small snapper fillets
	Paprika
1/2	cup port wine
4	tablespoons butter
1	tablespoon lemon or lime juice
2	tablespoons grated Parmesan cheese

Butter 4 individual 6 1/2 to 7" au gratin baking dishes. Arrange tomatoes in them. Sprinkle bread crumbs evenly over them and season with salt and pepper. Divide the snapper among the dishes. Combine port, lemon juice and butter in a small saucepan and heat until butter melts. Increase heat to moderate and boil 3 minutes. Pour over fish evenly. Sprinkle with the Parmesan and paprika to taste. Bake at 500° for 10 minutes. Makes 4 servings.

Ed Underhill
Original proprietor, The Unpressured Cooker

CRISPY SNAPPER WITH CONFETTI VEGGIES

1 1/2	tablespoons olive oil
1	clove garlic, minced (1 teaspoon)
1	red bell pepper, cored, seeded and minced
1	yellow bell pepper, cored, seeded and minced
1	small zucchini, cut in half lengthwise, seeded and minced
1	small yellow squash, cut in half lengthwise, seeded and minced
1/4	teaspoon saffron threads, soaked in 3 tablespoons hot water
1	teaspoon chopped fresh thyme (or 1 teaspoon dried)
	Salt, freshly ground black pepper and cayenne pepper
1 1/2	pounds snapper fillets, skins left on
1/2	cup (approximately) flour

Preheat oven to 400°. In a nonstick frying pan, heat 1/2 tablespoon oil. Add the garlic, peppers, zucchini and yellow squash; cook on high heat for 1 minute. Mix in the saffron, thyme, salt, pepper and cayenne. Reduce heat to medium; cook the veggies for 3 to 4 minutes until tender, but not soft. Adjust the seasoning with salt, pepper and cayenne to taste. The mixture should be very flavorful.

Cut the fish into 4 pieces and season with salt and pepper. Dredge in flour, shaking off any excess. Heat 1 tablespoon oil in an oven safe, nonstick frying pan. Add the fish, skin side down, and cook over medium heat until the skin is very crisp, about 3 to 4 minutes. Flip the fish and place the pan in the oven. Bake for 10 to 15 minutes until cooked. (When done, it will flake easily when pressed.) Place the fish, skin side up, on serving dishes. Spoon the veggie mixture around it and serve at once. Serves 4.

Kevin Pierce

COCONUT-GINGER RED SNAPPER
WITH MANGO SALAD

6	8-ounce red snapper fillets
1/2	cup coconut milk
1	teaspoon grated, peeled fresh gingerroot
1/2	teaspoon salt
	Pinch of cayenne pepper

MANGO SALAD:

1	tablespoon vegetable oil
1	tablespoon rice vinegar
1/2	teaspoon grated orange rind
1/4	teaspoon salt
2	mangoes, peeled and sliced
1	red bell pepper, cored, seeded and slivered
1/2	cup sliced scallions

Place fish in shallow glass baking dish. Combine coconut milk, gingerroot, salt and cayenne. Pour over fish and turn fish to coat; marinate for 30 minutes.

MANGO SALAD: Combine oil, vinegar, orange rind and salt; gently toss mango slices, red pepper and scallions with dressing to coat.

Remove fish from marinade and grill over low heat for 5 to 7 minutes, until cooked through. Serve with Mango Salad. Makes 6 servings.

GRILLED SWORDFISH WITH RED PEPPER AND PINEAPPLE SALSA

SALSA:
1   cup crushed pineapple (canned), including the juice
1   cup finely chopped red pepper
1/2   cup finely chopped coriander (cilantro)
     Juice of 1/2 a lime

FISH:
2   pounds fresh swordfish
     Olive oil
     Salt and pepper

Combine the salsa ingredients in a small bowl. Cover and refrigerate for at least 3 hours. Drizzle a small amount of olive oil over the fish and add salt and pepper to taste. Heat the grill. Place the fish directly on the grill and cook slowly for 3 to 4 minutes. Flip the fish and continue cooking until done, being careful to not overcook the fish. Remove the fish from the grill and serve topped with the salsa. Serves 4.

NOTE: This dish is virtually fat-free, so enjoy without feeling guilty!

Kitchen Tid-Bit:

Cutting a fresh pepper in half and trying to dig out the seeds and pulp can be a drag. Here's an easier way to eradicate those pesky little seeds: Cut both ends of the pepper. Stand the pepper on the counter and slice straight down with a sharp knife, removing the flesh in four or five pieces from around the core. Discard the seeds and the core and proceed, seed-free!

SEAFOOD CAKES
WITH JALAPENO TARTAR SAUCE

1/2	pound medium size fresh shrimp, peeled and deveined
1/2	pound grouper or other lean whitefish fillets
1/2	cup diced onion
1/4	cup diced celery
1/4	cup diced green bell pepper
1	tablespoon mayonnaise
1	tablespoon butter or margarine, melted
1	large egg
1	teaspoon Old Bay seasoning
2	teaspoons Worcestershire sauce
1/2	teaspoon paprika
1/4	teaspoon salt
1/4	teaspoon dried crushed red pepper
1/4	teaspoon ground black pepper
1/2	pound fresh crab meat, drained and flaked (or 1 6-ounce can lump crab meat, drained)
3	cups soft bread crumbs, divided
2	tablespoons butter or margarine
2	tablespoons vegetable oil
	Jalapeno Tartar Sauce

Steam shrimp and grouper in a steamer basket until the grouper flakes easily with a fork, about 10 minutes. Cool and chop the grouper and shrimp. Combine the next 12 ingredients; stir in the shrimp mixture, crab meat and 1 cup bread crumbs. Form the mixture into 12 patties and coat with the remaining 2 cups of bread crumbs. Cover and chill 1 hour. Heat the remaining butter and oil in a large skillet over medium heat. Add patties and cook until golden brown, about 3 minutes on each side. Drain on paper towels and serve with Jalapeno Tartar Sauce. Serves 6.

JALAPENO TARTAR SAUCE:

1	cup reduced-fat mayonnaise
1	jalapeno pepper, diced
2	tablespoons sweet pickle relish
1	tablespoon chopped fresh or frozen chives
1	tablespoon capers
1	teaspoon dried dill weed

Combine all ingredients. Cover and chill.

CABBAGE KEY CONCOCTION

1/2	cup diced salt pork
1/2	cup diced ham
1/2	cup chopped onion
1	clove garlic, crushed
1	tablespoon diced green pepper
2	cups canned tomatoes
1	small red pepper pod, finely chopped
2	tablespoons chopped parsley
1/2	bay leaf, crushed
1	cup uncooked rice
1	cup water
1	pint fresh oysters
1	pint raw shrimp, shelled

Saute salt pork and ham slowly in heavy skillet until crisp. Add onion, garlic and green pepper; cook until onion is transparent. Add tomatoes, red pepper, parsley and bay leaf. Simmer, stirring frequently, until thick. Add rice and water. Cover and simmer until rice is just tender. Add oysters and shrimp. Cook only until oysters curl and shrimp are pink. Makes 6 servings.

Carol Zook

FRUITS DE MER

3	raw lobster tails, 1 pound
1/4	pound bay scallops
2	cups light cream
1	cup sliced mushrooms
1/2	cup vermouth or white wine
4	tablespoons flour
3	tablespoons sherry
	Salt
1	pound raw shrimp
1	cup fresh oysters
1/4	pound butter
1	clove garlic, minced
2	tablespoons sherry
2	tablespoons creme fraiche or heavy cream
1	tablespoon cognac
	Pepper

Shell lobster tails and remove vein; cut into slices 1/2" thick; set aside. Clean shrimp, shell and devein; add to lobster tails. Wash scallops and oysters in the 2 cups cream; set aside. Strain cream through fine sieve or dampened cloth. Melt butter in skillet. Add lobster tails, shrimp and scallops to butter; heat. Add mushrooms, garlic, vermouth and 2 tablespoons sherry. Stir with wooden spoon. Bring to boil, reduce heat and simmer 3 minutes. Lift seafoods out of liquid to plate with oysters. Boil liquid reducing it down to the butter. Stir in flour and cook a few minutes. Add strained light cream and cook until thickened. Add oysters and scallops. Add about 1/2 cup sauce to creme then stir into pan. Add 3 tablespoons sherry and cognac. Season, taste and adjust seasonings.

NOTE: Creme fraiche is 1 cup whipping cream and 3 tablespoons yogurt.

Alice MacKenzie

Notes

MEALS FOR THE MILLENNIUM

*From Appetizers to Desserts
in the Microwave and Crock Pot*

MANGO CHUTNEY

Preparation time: 10 minutes.

1	mango
1/2	cup sugar
1/4	cup finely chopped red onion
2	tablespoons white vinegar
2	tablespoons finely chopped green pepper
1	tablespoon grated fresh ginger
1/2	teaspoon ground ginger
1/8	teaspoon ground cloves
	Freshly ground black pepper to taste
1/8	teaspoon ground turmeric

Peel, halve and seed the mango, cut into 1/2" cubes. Combine the mango with all the other ingredients in a deep 1 1/2-quart, microwave-safe casserole; stir thoroughly. Cook, uncovered, at full power (650 to 700 watts) for 7 minutes. Allow the chutney to cool slightly; then cover tightly and refrigerate. It will keep for 1 week in the refrigerator. Makes 1 cup.

Liz Fowler

CROCK POT CHICKEN WINGS

3	pounds chicken wings
1 1/2	cups bottled barbecue sauce
1/4	cup honey
2	teaspoons prepared mustard
1 1/2	teaspoons Worcestershire sauce

Rinse chicken and pat dry. Cut off and discard wing tips. Cut each wing at joint to make 2 sections. Place chicken on the unheated rack of a broiler pan. Broil 4 to 5" from heat about 10 minutes until chicken is browned, turning once. Transfer chicken to a crock pot. Combine barbecue sauce, honey, mustard and Worcestershire sauce. Pour over chicken wings. Cover and cook on low for 4 to 5 hours or on high for 2 to 2 1/2 hours. Makes about 32 appetizers.

SHRIMP PATÉ

3/4	pound shrimp, shelled and deveined
1 1/2	cups heavy cream
1	tablespoon fresh lemon juice
3/4	teaspoon kosher salt
1/8	teaspoon cayenne pepper
	Freshly ground black pepper

Line a 7x3 1/2" loaf pan with microwave plastic wrap, leaving a 4" overhang around top. Place the shrimp in the work bowl of a food processor and puree until coarse, scraping down sides of bowl several times. Combine cream with remaining ingredients. With the processor motor running, add to shrimp puree in a thin stream. Continue processing until the cream is incorporated and the mixture is very smooth, about 1 minute. Don't overprocess, as the cream will curdle. Pour mixture into prepared loaf pan. Fold over plastic wrap to enclose paté. Cook at 100 percent power for 4 minutes. Remove from oven. Uncover and wrap the loaf pan in a kitchen towel. Let stand for 20 minutes. Unmold on a serving plate and serve warm or cool.

BASIC BROCCOLI
WITH CHEDDAR CHEESE SAUCE

BROCCOLI:

2 1/2	pounds broccoli, trimmed of leaves and cut into 4-5" stalks with florets
1/4	cup water
	Kosher salt
	Fresh lemon juice

Arrange broccoli in a single layer, spoke-fashion with florets pointing toward center of a 12" round platter. Pour water over broccoli. Cover tightly with microwave plastic wrap and cook at 100% power for 12 minutes. Remove from oven. Uncover and add salt and lemon juice.

SAUCE:

1/2	cup milk
2 1/2	cups grated Cheddar cheese
	Kosher salt
	Freshly ground black pepper

Heat milk in a 2-cup glass measure, uncovered, at 100% power for 1 minute. Remove from oven. Add cheese and stir to moisten. Scrape mixture into a blender or food processor and puree until smooth. Return to 2-cup measure. Heat, uncovered, at 100% power for 30 seconds. Remove from oven and stir. Pour over broccoli and serve.

Cindy Pierce

SZECHUAN GREEN BEANS

6   cloves garlic, smashed and peeled
2   quarter size slices fresh ginger, peeled
2   scallions, trimmed and cut into 2"
      lengths
1   tablespoon vegetable oil
1   teaspoon hot red pepper flakes
1   tablespoon tamari soy
1   tablespoon rice wine vinegar
1   pound green beans, tipped and tailed

In a food processor, process garlic, ginger and scallions until finely chopped. Remove to a 14x11x2" casserole. Add oil and pepper flakes. Cook, uncovered, at 100% power for 3 minutes. Remove from oven. Stir in remaining ingredients. Cook, uncovered, at 100% power for 15 minutes, stirring every 3 to 4 minutes. Remove from oven. Stir and serve hot or cold.

Kevin Pierce

DILLED BARLEY VEGETABLE SOUP

1	15-ounce can red beans, drained
1	10-ounce package frozen whole kernel corn
1/2	cup medium pearl barley
1	14 1/2-ounce can stewed tomatoes
2	cups sliced fresh mushrooms
1	cup chopped onion
1	medium carrot, coarsely chopped
1	stalk celery, coarsely chopped
3	cloves garlic, minced
2	teaspoons dried dill weed
1/4	teaspoon pepper
1	bay leaf
5	cups vegetable broth or chicken broth

In a 3 1/2-, 4- or 5-quart crockery cooker, place beans, corn, barley, undrained tomatoes, mushrooms, onion, carrot, celery, garlic, dill weed, pepper and bay leaf. Pour broth over all. Cover; cook on low-heat setting for 8 to 10 hours or on high-heat setting for 4 to 5 hours. Discard bay leaf. Makes 6 servings.

Liz Fowler

QUICK CHICKEN AND RICE
(LOADED WITH GARLIC!)

1	chicken, about 4 1/2 pounds, cut into serving pieces
2 to 3	heads garlic, cloves smashed and peeled
2 1/2	cups chicken broth
	Freshly ground black pepper
1	cup long-grain rice
1	package tiny frozen peas
2	teaspoons kosher salt

Arrange chicken, skin side down, in a 2-quart souffle; place breasts in center of dish with legs, thighs, wings and back around them. Scatter garlic over and pour 1 1/2 cups of the broth all over. Sprinkle with pepper. Cover tightly with microwave plastic wrap and cook at 100% power for 20 minutes. Remove from oven and uncover. Remove chicken and keep warm. Strain cooking liquid into a 2-cup glass measure and add broth to make 2 cups. Bring cooking liquid and broth to a boil in a saucepan on the stove. Add rice and cook. When done, add peas, chicken and salt. Heat through and serve.

ORANGE TERIYAKI CHICKEN

1	pound skinless, boneless chicken breast halves or thighs
1	16-ounce package loose-pack frozen broccoli, baby carrots and water chestnuts
2	tablespoons quick-cooking tapioca
1/2	cup chicken broth
2	tablespoons brown sugar
2	tablespoons teriyaki sauce
1	teaspoon dry mustard
1	teaspoon finely shredded orange peel
1/2	teaspoon ground ginger
2	cups hot cooked rice

Rinse chicken pat dry. Cut chicken into 1" pieces. In a 3 1/2-, 4- or 5-quart crockery cooker, place frozen vegetables. Sprinkle tapioca over vegetables. Place chicken pieces atop vegetables.

For sauce, in a small bowl, combine chicken broth, brown sugar, teriyaki sauce, mustard, orange peel and ginger.

Pour sauce over chicken pieces. Cover; cook on low-heat setting for 4 to 6 hours or on high-heat setting for 2 to 3 hours. Serve with hot cooked rice. Serves 4.

PORK CHOPS WITH APPLES AND SAUERKRAUT

Try pork spareribs for a variation of this mouth-watering meat. Rinse and drain the sauerkraut if you prefer a milder flavor.

4	pork sirloin chops (about 1 1/2 pounds), cut 3/4" thick
4	medium carrots, cut into 1/2" pieces
1	tablespoon cooking oil
1	medium onion, thinly sliced
1	16-ounce can sauerkraut, drained
2	small cooking apples, cut into 1/4" slices
1/2	cup apple cider or apple juice
1/4	cup catsup
1/2	teaspoon caraway seed
	Snipped fresh parsley (optional)

In a large skillet, brown pork chops on both sides in hot oil. In a 3 1/2- or 4-quart crockery cooker, place carrots, onion, browned pork chops, sauerkraut and apples. In a bowl, combine apple cider or apple juice, catsup and caraway seed; pour over apples. Cover; cook on low-heat setting for 6 to 8 hours or on high-heat setting for 3 or 4 hours. Garnish with snipped fresh parsley, if desired. Makes 4 servings.

Liz Fowler

SATURDAY NIGHT BAKED BEANS

3 1/2	cups dry kidney beans
1/2	pound bacon, cut in 1" pieces
1	medium to large onion, chopped
1/2	cup packed brown sugar
1/2	cup real maple syrup
1	teaspoon salt
1	cup water
1	teaspoon dry mustard
2/3	cup catsup
2	tablespoons prepared mustard

Put dry beans in large pot and cover with 3 times their volume of unsalted water. Bring to a boil and continue to boil for 10 minutes. Reduce heat, cover and simmer until beans are tender (about 1 hour). Drain beans and put into crock pot. Add all other ingredients along with 1 cup of water; mix well. Cover and cook on low 10 to 12 hours or on high for 4 to 5 hours. During the last hour of cooking, stir in 2/3 cup catsup and 2 tablespoons prepared mustard.

Jo Caldwell

SPICY SOUTHWESTERN BEEF STEW

If jalapeno pinto beans are not available in your area, add 1 finely chopped jalapeno pepper.

1	pound beef chuck pot roast
1	tablespoon cooking oil
2	14 1/2-ounce cans Mexican style stewed tomatoes
1 1/2	cups coarsely chopped onion
1	15-ounce can pinto beans or jalapeno pinto beans
3 1/2	cups beef broth
1	6-ounce can tomato paste
4	teaspoons chili powder
4	teaspoons dried Italian seasoning, crushed
1/2	teaspoon crushed red pepper
1/4	teaspoon ground cloves
1/4	teaspoon ground allspice
1/4	teaspoon ground cinnamon
1	medium zucchini, halved lengthwise and cut into 1/2" pieces
1	medium yellow or green sweet pepper, cut into 1" pieces

Trim fat from meat. Cut meat into 1" cubes. In a large skillet, brown meat, half at a time, in hot oil. Drain off fat. Transfer meat to a 3 1/2-, 4- or 5-quart crockery cooker. Add undrained tomatoes, onion and beans. In a bowl, combine beef broth, tomato paste, chili powder, Italian seasoning, crushed red pepper, cloves, allspice and cinnamon. Add to cooker. Cover; cook on low-heat setting for 10 to 12 hours or on high-heat setting for 5 to 6 hours. After stew is cooked, if low-heat setting was used, turn to high-heat setting. Add zucchini and sweet peppers. Cover and cook 30 minutes longer on high-heat setting. Makes 6 servings.

NOTE: For a milder taste, substitute 1 can corn for chili powder and red peppers.

Liz Fowler

BARBECUE-STYLE RIBS

3 to 3 1/2	pounds pork country style ribs, cut crosswise in half and cut into 2-rib portions
1	cup catsup
1/2	cup finely chopped onion
1/4	cup packed brown sugar
1	tablespoon Worcestershire sauce
1/2	teaspoon chili powder
1/4	teaspoon liquid smoke
1/4	teaspoon garlic powder
1/4	teaspoon bottled hot pepper sauce

Preheat broiler. Place ribs on the unheated rack of a broiler pan. Broil 6" from the heat until brown, about 10 minutes, turning once. Transfer ribs to a 3 1/2- to 4-quart crockery cooker. In a small bowl, combine catsup, onion, brown sugar, Worcestershire sauce, chili powder, liquid smoke, garlic powder and bottled hot pepper sauce. Pour sauce over ribs, turning to coat. Cover; cook on low-heat setting for 10 to 12 hours or on high-heat setting for 5 to 6 hours. Transfer ribs to a platter. If desired, skim fat from surface of sauce; pour sauce into a medium saucepan. Simmer sauce until reduced and thickened. Pass sauce with ribs. Makes 4 servings.

Kathy Pierce

SOUTH-OF-THE-BORDER BEEF FAJITAS

1 1/2	pounds beef flank steak
1	cup chopped onion
1	green sweet pepper, cut into 1/2" pieces
1 or 2	jalapeno peppers, chopped
1	tablespoon snipped fresh cilantro
2	gloves garlic, minced
1	teaspoon chili powder
1	teaspoon ground cumin
1	teaspoon ground coriander
1/4	teaspoon salt
1	8-ounce can stewed tomatoes
12	flour tortillas
2 to 3	teaspoons lime juice (optional)
	Shredded Co-Jack cheese (optional)
	Guacamole (optional)
	Dairy sour cream (optional)
	Salsa (optional)

Trim fat from meat. Cut flank steak into 6 portions. In a 3 1/2-quart crockery cooker, combine meat, onion, green sweet pepper, jalapeno pepper(s), cilantro, garlic, chili powder, cumin, coriander and salt. Add undrained tomatoes. Cover; cool on low-heat setting for 8 to 10 hours or on high-heat setting 4 to 5 hours.

To heat tortillas, wrap them in foil and place in 350° oven for 10 to 15 minutes or until softened.

Remove meat from cooker and shred. Return meat to cooker. Stir in lime juice, if desired.

To serve fajitas, use a slotted spoon and fill the warmed tortillas with the beef mixture. If desired, add shredded cheese, guacamole, sour cream, and salsa. Roll up tortillas. Makes 6 servings.

Liz Fowler

SHRIMP AND SPRING VEGETABLE RISOTTO

3	tablespoons unsalted butter
3	tablespoons olive oil
1/2	cup chopped scallion, white part only
2	celery stalks, peeled and chopped
1/2	cup chopped parsley
2	cups arborio or short-grain rice
4	cups clam broth or chicken broth
3/4	pound asparagus, trimmed, peeled and cut into 2" lengths
1	pound medium shrimp, peeled, deveined and cut in half crosswise
3/4	cup frozen peas
1 to 2	teaspoons kosher salt
1/2	teaspoon freshly ground black pepper
1/4	cup chopped scallion, green part only
1/2	cup freshly grated Parmesan cheese

Heat butter and oil in a 14x11x2" casserole, uncovered, at 100% power for 3 minutes. Add scallion whites, celery, parsley and rice; stir to coat. Cook, uncovered, at 100% power for 4 minutes. Stir in broth and cook, uncovered, at 100% power for 12 minutes. Add asparagus, shrimp and peas; stir well. Cook, uncovered, at 100% power for 12 minutes more. Remove from oven. Stir in salt and pepper. Cover loosely with paper towels and let stand for 8 to 10 minutes. Uncover, sprinkle with scallion greens and Parmesan; serve.

Kevin Pierce

STRAWBERRY-RHUBARB COMPOTE

6   cups fresh rhubarb, cut into 1" pieces (about 2 pounds) or 1 20-ounce package frozen unsweetened sliced rhubarb
1   cup sugar
1/2   teaspoon finely shredded orange peel or lemon peel
1/4   teaspoon ground ginger
1   3-inch stick cinnamon
1/2   cup white grape juice, white wine or water
2   cups fresh strawberries, halved or quartered
   Vanilla ice cream or frozen yogurt

In a 3 1/2- or 4-quart crockery cooker, place rhubarb. In a bowl, combine sugar, orange or lemon peel and ginger; sprinkle over rhubarb. Add cinnamon stick. Pour grape juice, wine or water over all. Cover; cook on low-heat setting for 5 to 6 hours or on high-setting for 2 1/2 to 3 hours. Remove stick cinnamon. If using low-heat setting, turn to high-heat setting. Stir in strawberries. Cover and cook 30 minutes longer on high-heat setting. Spoon the warm compote into dishes. Serve with ice cream or yogurt. Makes 4 to 6 servings.

Liz Fowler

MEXICAN CHOCOLATE BREAD PUDDING

1 1/2	cups half and half or light cream
3	ounces unsweetened chocolate, coarsely chopped
1/3	cup raisins (optional)
2	beaten eggs
1/2	cup sugar
3/4	teaspoon ground cinnamon
3	cups 1/2" bread cubes (about 4 slices)
	Whipped cream (optional)
	Chopped nuts (optional)

In a small saucepan, heat cream over medium heat until steaming. Remove from heat and add chopped chocolate and raisins. Stir occasionally until chocolate melts. In a medium bowl, whisk together eggs, sugar and cinnamon. Whisk in cream mixture. Gently stir in bread crumbs. Pour into a 1-quart souffle dish. Cover the dish tightly with foil. Tear off two 15x6" pieces of heavy foil. Fold each piece in thirds lengthwise. Crisscross the strips and place the souffle dish in the center. Bring up foil strips, lift the ends of the strips and transfer the dish and foil to a 3 1/2-, 4- or 5-quart crockery cooker. (Leave foil strips under dish.) Pour warm water into the cooker around the dish to a depth of 2" (about 1 cup). Cover; cook on low-heat setting about 4 hours or on high-heat setting about 2 hours or until a knife inserted near the center comes out clean. Using foil strips, carefully lift the dish out of cooker. Serve bread pudding warm or chilled. If desired, top each serving with a dollop of whipped cream and sprinkle with nuts. Makes 6 servings.

Cindy Pierce

8-MINUTE COMPANY BROWNIES

1/2	pound unsalted butter
2	ounces unsweetened chocolate
1	ounce semi-sweet chocolate
1/4	cup granulated sugar
1	cup (packed) light brown sugar
2	eggs
1	teaspoon vanilla extract
	Pinch of kosher salt
1/4	teaspoon baking powder
3/4	cup cake flour, sifted

Place butter and all chocolate in an 8-cup glass measure. Cover tightly with microwave plastic wrap. Cook at 100% power for 2 minutes. Remove from oven. Uncover and whisk until combined. Whisk in all sugar and then eggs, one at a time. Stir in vanilla. Sift together salt, baking powder and flour. Fold into chocolate mixture. Pour into an 8" square or oval dish. Cover tightly with microwave plastic wrap. Cook at 100% for 4 minutes. Uncover and cook for 2 minutes longer. Remove from oven. Cut into squares and let stand until cool.

CHUNKY FUDGE BROWNIES: When folding in dry ingredients, stir in 1/3 cup raisins and 1/3 cup coarsely chopped walnuts. Follow cooking instructions above.

Cindy Pierce

Notes

CASA YBEL COOKIES AND PERIWINKLE PIES

Sweet Treats and Decadent Desserts

UNBELIEVABLE VELVEETA CHEESE FUDGE

1	pound butter
1	pound Velveeta cheese
4	pounds powdered sugar
1	cup cocoa
1	tablespoon vanilla
12	ounces nuts

Melt butter and cheese over medium heat until smooth. Add vanilla. Mix cocoa and sugar and add cheese mixture to dry ingredients; mix well. Stir in nuts. Press into pan. Cool before cutting into squares.

NOTE: This recipe makes two 9x13" pans and is great for the holidays.

Karen Lund

BAKLAVA

FILLING:
1   pound unsalted butter
1   pound filo dough
1   pound blanched almonds, chopped fine
1   teaspoon cinnamon
1/2 cup sugar

SYRUP:
3   cups sugar
1   cup water
    Juice of 1/2 a lemon
    Lemon rind

Mix almonds, sugar and cinnamon together to make nut filling. In a pan, 13x9", brush bottom with melted butter. Add 6 layers of filo, brush each sheet. With your hands, sprinkle enough nut filling to lightly cover top filo sheet. Add 4 more filo layers, brushing each layer and sprinkling nut filling on top. Continue until at least a dozen sheets are left for top. Be sure to brush each layer with butter. Before baking, take a sharp knife and cut the baklava into squares, 1 1/2x1 1/2". Be careful not to cut into bottom layers of filo dough. Bake at 375° until top is golden brown, about 1 hour. While pastry is baking, make a syrup. Cook until thick; cool. Pour over hot baklava. Serve at room temperature or cool.

HINT: For best results, syrup should be cold and thick.

Eugenia Kontinos Loughney
Co-chair, 1st edition
Sanibel-Captiva Cookbook

BANANA OATMEAL COOKIES
(LOADED WITH FIBER!)

3/4	cup butter, softened
1/2	cup sugar
1/2	cup firmly packed brown sugar
1	egg
1 1/2	cups all-purpose flour
1	teaspoon salt
1/2	teaspoon nutmeg
1/2	teaspoon cinnamon
1/2	teaspoon cloves
1	teaspoon baking powder
1	cup rolled oats
2	large ripe bananas, coarsely mashed
1	teaspoon vanilla extract

Preheat oven to 375°. In a large bowl, cream butter with an electric mixer. Beat in sugars until well mixed. Add egg and beat until fluffy. Add flour, spices and baking powder, beating until thoroughly mixed. Mix in oats, mashed bananas and vanilla. Drop by tablespoon 2" apart onto a greased cookie sheet. Bake for 12 to 15 minutes until golden. Remove to rack to cool.

Nancy Gerhard

SAM'S CARDAMOM BARS

1	cup softened butter
1/2	cup sugar
1/2	cup brown sugar, packed
1	egg, separated
1	teaspoon vanilla or almond extract
2	cups flour
1	teaspoon ground cardamom
1/4	teaspoon salt
1/3	cup chopped nuts

Cream butter and sugars; add egg yolk, vanilla, flour, cardamom and salt. Mix well to form a soft dough. Spread into an ungreased 10x15" pan. Brush with beaten egg white and sprinkle with nuts. Bake at 275° for 1 hour. Drizzle with the following frosting while still warm. Makes 4 dozen.

FROSTING FOR CARDAMOM BARS:

1 1/2	tablespoons butter
1	cup powdered sugar
1/2	teaspoon vanilla
	Milk

Melt and slightly brown the butter. Combine with powdered sugar, vanilla and enough milk for drizzling consistency.

Karen Halverson

HILLARY CLINTON'S CHEWY CHOCOLATE CHIP COOKIES

1 1/2	cups unsifted all-purpose flour
1	teaspoon salt
1	teaspoon baking soda
1	cup solid shortening (Crisco works great)
1/2	cup granulated sugar
1	cup firmly packed light brown sugar
1	teaspoon vanilla extract
2	eggs
2	cups old-fashioned rolled oats
12	ounce package semi-sweet chocolate chips (we like Nestle's)

Preheat oven to 350°. Combine flour, salt and baking soda. Beat together shortening, sugars and vanilla until creamy. Add eggs, beating until light and fluffy. Gradually beat in flour mixture and rolled oats. Stir in chocolate chips. Drop batter by well-rounded teaspoonfuls onto cooking sheets. Bake 8 to 10 minutes or until cookies are done. Don't let them get too brown! Cool on cookie sheets for a couple of minutes before placing them on wire racks for further cooling. Yields about 7 dozen cookies.

Cindy Pierce

CHEWY COCONUT COOKIES

1 1/2	sticks margarine
2	cups light brown sugar
2	eggs, beaten slightly
1	cup coconut
1	cup flour
1	teaspoon vanilla
1/8	teaspoon salt

Cream margarine and sugar slightly. Add eggs, then remaining ingredients. Bake in greased 12x6" pan at 325° for 40 to 45 minutes or until done. Cut while warm, but leave in pan until cool. Makes about 28.

NOTE: These are chewy, moist and delicious.

Van Hooper

Quotable Kid:

Never touch a cookie
when it's in the oven.
Micaela, 4

RAMSEY'S GRANDMOM'S
COCOA DROP COOKIES

1	cup sugar
2/3	cup butter or margarine
1	egg
1/2	cup cocoa
1/3	cup water
1	teaspoon vanilla
1 3/4	cups flour
1/2	teaspoon baking soda
1/2	teaspoon salt

Mix all ingredients and form into balls. Enjoy!

Maxine Fisher

GINGER COOKIES

3/4	cup Crisco
1	cup sugar
1	egg
1/4	cup gold label molasses
2	cups flour, sifted
2	teaspoons baking soda
1/2	teaspoon salt
1/2	teaspoon ginger
1/2	teaspoon cloves
1	teaspoon cinnamon

Combine Crisco, sugar, egg, molasses and mix well. Sift dry ingredients together. Add to molasses mixture; mix. Chill dough in refrigerator. When ready to bake, form into 1" balls and dip in granulated sugar. Bake at 375° for 8 to 10 minutes.

NOTE: The dough may be kept in refrigerator and used "as needed."

Cort Daniels

GINGERBREAD COOKIES

1 1/2	cups shortening, melt and cool
2	cups sugar
1/2	cup molasses
2	eggs
4 3/4	cups flour
1	teaspoon ginger
2	teaspoons cinnamon
1	teaspoon cloves
4	teaspoons baking soda
1	teaspoon salt

Add sugar, molasses and eggs to cooled shortening. Add dry ingredients; mix well. Chill dough. Form into balls and roll in sugar. Flatten slightly with fork. Bake at 375° for 8 to 10 minutes. Let cool before removing from baking sheets. Serve on a chilly fall day with a cup of fresh brewed coffee.

Sharon Chamberlain

Quotable Kid:

A good rule is no fingers in the blender.
Jamie, 6

LEMON SQUARES

2	cups flour
1	cup butter or oleo
2/3	cup powdered sugar
4	eggs
2	cups sugar
1/2	teaspoon salt
1/2	teaspoon baking powder
3	tablespoons lemon juice

Mix first 3 ingredients well and flatten into 9x9" pan. Bake for 15 minutes at 350°. Combine eggs, sugar, salt, baking powder and lemon juice. Beat well and pour over hot crust and bake for 25 minutes. Sprinkle with powdered sugar and cut when cool.

Mozella Jordan

MONSTER COOKIES
(BIG...AND PLENTIFUL!)

12	eggs
2	pounds brown sugar
4	cups white sugar
1	tablespoon vanilla extract
1	tablespoon corn syrup
8	teaspoons baking soda
1	pound butter
3	pounds peanut butter
18	cups oatmeal
1	pound chocolate chips
1	pound M & M's plain chocolate candy

Mix all ingredients in a large mixing bowl. This makes a ton of cookies. Make them huge, that's the fun part.

NEED 'EMS
(TAD'S DAD'S FAVORITE)

1/4	cup butter
3/4	cup mashed potatoes
1/2	teaspoon salt
2	pounds confectioners' sugar
1	large bag shredded coconut
2	teaspoons vanilla

Melt butter in double boiler. Add all ingredients; mix well. Spread on a large pan and refrigerate to harden. Cut in bars and insert toothpick in each piece to dunk into chocolate batter.

1	12-ounce package chocolate bits
4	squares unsweetened chocolate
1/2	cake paraffin wax

Melt in a double boiler. Dip bars into chocolate and place on waxed paper. Let harden before serving.

Jo Caldwell

NO BAKE PEANUT BUTTER SQUARES

1/2	cup chunky peanut butter
1 1/3	cups granulated sugar
1/3	cup cocoa
1/4	cup butter
1/2	cup milk
3	cups quick, cooking oatmeal
2	teaspoons vanilla

Mix sugar and cocoa in saucepan; add butter and milk. Bring to the boiling point, stirring constantly. Simmer 2 minutes. Remove from heat and stir in oats, vanilla and peanut butter; mix well. Pour into buttered square pan; cool. Cut into squares.

Ede Stokes

EMMA'S BEST PEANUT BUTTER BUCKEYES

1 1/3	sticks margarine
1	12-ounce jar creamy peanut butter
16	ounces powdered sugar
3	Hershey bars
6	ounces chocolate chips
	Paraffin

Mix margarine, peanut butter and powdered sugar; form into balls. Put on cookie sheet in freezer while preparing chocolate dip. Melt Hershey bars and chocolate chips with a pinch of paraffin (about 3 or 4 shavings with a vegetable peeler) in a double boiler. Using a toothpick, dip the balls halfway into the chocolate. Set onto waxed paper until set.

NOTE: Paraffin helps chocolate hold its shape. It can be found in grocery stores with home canning supplies.

Karen Halverson

SNICKERDOODLES

1	cup shortening
1 1/2	cups sugar
2	eggs
2 2/3	cups sifted flour
3	teaspoons cream of tartar
1	teaspoon baking soda
1/4	teaspoon salt
3	tablespoons sugar
3	teaspoons cinnamon

Combine the shortening, sugar, eggs, flour, cream of tartar, baking soda and salt. Roll into balls about the size of a walnut; coat with mixture of sugar and cinnamon. Bake on an ungreased cookie sheet at 400° for 8 to 10 minutes.

Jean Dutton

APPLE SLUMP

Preheat oven to 350°.

5 to 6	large apples, sliced
2	cups sugar
	Cinnamon and nutmeg
1	cup hot water

Line a baking dish with the apple slices and sprinkle with sugar, spices and water.

2	cups flour
4	teaspoons baking powder
1	teaspoon salt
4	tablespoons shortening

Mix the above ingredients with just enough milk to make a soft biscuit dough. Drop dough by the spoonful onto the apples and sugar. Bake for 30 to 35 minutes. Serve warm with vanilla ice cream.

Jo Caldwell

BUTTERNUT-APPLE CRISP

1/2	cup packed brown sugar
1	teaspoon cinnamon
1	butternut squash, pared and sliced
1/2	cup flour
1/4	cup packed brown sugar
2	tablespoons lemon juice
1/2	teaspoon salt
1	20-ounce can apples, undrained
1/2	cup quick cooking oats
6	tablespoons butter

Mix brown sugar, lemon juice, cinnamon and salt. Add squash, which has been pared, quartered, seeded and sliced and apples which have not been drained. Toss gently to coat. Turn mixture into baking dish. Bake, covered, at 375° for 30 minutes in medium casserole. Combine flour, oats, brown sugar and butter. Cut in the butter until the mixture resembles crumbs. Sprinkle over the squash and bake at 375°, uncovered, until the top is browned. Makes 6 to 8 servings.

Faye Wollenberg

CRANBERRY APPLE CRISP

3	cups apples, sliced
2	cups whole fresh or frozen cranberries
2	tablespoons honey
1/2	cup butter
1	cup rolled oats
1/2	cup whole wheat flour
3/4	cup brown sugar
1/2	cup chopped nuts
1/2	teaspoon vanilla

Combine apple slices and cranberries. Drizzle with honey; toss lightly. Cut butter into oats, flour and sugar; mix until crumbly. Stir in nuts and vanilla. Place fruit in greased 9x13" pan. Sprinkle oat mixture over fruit and bake at 350° for 50 minutes or until brown and bubbly.

Pam Pfahler

CORNMEAL-CRUSTED SUMMER COBBLER
(TWO THUMBS UP FROM KARI AND SAM!)

Muffin-like batter tops the fruit filling of this easier-than-pie dessert. Add a heaping spoonful of frozen vanilla yogurt or ice cream for guaranteed satisfaction!

FILLING:

2 1/2	pounds nectarines (about 10 small), unpeeled but pitted and sliced
3	red plums, unpeeled but pitted and sliced
1/3	cup sugar
1	tablespoon cornstarch
2	tablespoons honey
1/2	pint blackberries

NOTE: A combination of peaches, plums and blueberries is equally delicious!

TOPPING:

1/2	cup yellow cornmeal
1/2	cup all-purpose flour
1/4	cup sugar
1 1/2	teaspoons baking powder
1/4	teaspoon cinnamon
1/4	teaspoon salt
1	large egg
1/2	cup buttermilk
2	tablespoons melted butter
1	teaspoon vanilla extract

Heat oven to 400°. Lightly butter a 2-quart baking dish.

FILLING: Toss together the nectarines, plums, sugar and cornstarch. Stir in honey. Gently fold in the berries. Turn mixture into the prepared dish.

TOPPING: Combine the cornmeal, flour, sugar, baking powder, cinnamon and salt until well mixed. In a separate bowl, whisk together the egg, buttermilk, butter and vanilla; stir into the flour mixture just until combined and thick batter formed. Spoon batter randomly on top of filling, leaving some parts of the filling uncovered. Bake cobbler 25 to 30 minutes or until filling is bubbly and top is lightly browned. Cool at least 30 minutes before serving. Serves 8.

Liz Fowler

GRILLED PEACHES WITH RASPBERRY PUREE

1/2	10-ounce package frozen raspberries in light syrup, slightly thawed
1 1/2	teaspoons lemon juice
2	medium peaches, peeled, halved and pitted
1 1/2	tablespoons brown sugar
1/4	teaspoon ground cinnamon
1 1/2	teaspoons rum flavoring
2	teaspoons butter

Combine raspberries and lemon juice; process in blender until smooth. Strain the puree and discard the seeds. Cover and chill. Cut an 18x18" sheet of heavy-duty aluminum foil. Place peach halves, cut side up, on foil. Combine brown sugar and cinnamon; spoon evenly onto center of each peach half. Sprinkle with rum flavoring and dot with butter. Fold foil over peaches and loosely seal. Place grill rack over medium coals. Place peach bundle on rack and cook 15 minutes or until peaches are thoroughly heated. To serve, spoon 2 tablespoons raspberry puree over each grilled peach half. Serves 4.

ORANGES IN COINTREAU

This recipe comes from South Africa via Atlanta. It's a "fancy" but light-tasting dessert that's really easy to make and serve for a buffet.

12 to 15	navel oranges, peeled and sliced or segmented
1 1/2	cups sugar
1 1/2	cups water
1 1/2	cups cane sugar syrup (Karo syrup)
1/4	cup lemon juice
1/4	cup Cointreau

Place the orange segments in a large jar or other sealable container such as Tupperware. Combine next 3 ingredients in saucepan and bring to a boil. Stir until sugar is dissolved. Cover over medium heat, uncovered, for 40 minutes until slightly thickened. Remove from heat. Stir in lemon juice and liqueur. Pour over oranges and refrigerate at least overnight. Serve cold.

Susan Wener

OLD ISLAND DELIGHT

6	halved bananas
3/4	cup dark brown sugar
1/2	cup dry bread or white cake crumbs
1/4	teaspoon cinnamon
3/4	cup fresh orange juice
1/2	cup grated coconut
1/4	teaspoon nutmeg

Place bananas in buttered baking dish. Mix orange juice and sugar; pour over bananas. Mix crumbs, coconut and spices. Sprinkle over top and bake in 325° oven for 15 to 20 minutes. Makes 6 servings.

June Holland

MANGO SURPRISE

2	cups fruit, sliced
1/2	cup brown sugar
8	pats butter
2	cups self-rising flour
1	stick butter, softened
1 1/2	cups sugar
2	eggs
3/4	cup buttermilk
1 1/2	teaspoons vanilla

Mix fruit and brown sugar, pour into oiled and floured 9" pan. Lay pats of butter over fruit; set aside. (Cake is mixed in 1 bowl.) Mix butter, sugar, vanilla and eggs well. Add flour alternately with buttermilk, pour over fruit, bake in oven, preheated to 350°, for 1 hour. (Oven heat varies, check after 45 minutes.) Other fruits can be substituted. Makes 18 (1 1/2" squares) servings.

Lola Bowers

KEY LIME CAKE PUDDING

1/2	cup sugar
3	tablespoons melted margarine
3	tablespoons freshly squeezed key lime juice
1	cup milk
3	tablespoons all-purpose flour
2	eggs, separated
1	teaspoon grated Key lime rind
	Whipped cream (optional)

Combine sugar, flour and melted margarine in a mixing bowl. Add the unbeaten egg yolks, lime juice and rind and milk. Beat egg whites until stiff and fold into yolk mixture. Pour into a greased 1-quart mold or 6 custard cups. Place in pan of hot water and bake at 325° for 1 hour or until the pudding leaves the sides of the mold (35 minutes for custard cups).

NOTE: The finished pudding has a cake-like top with a smooth lime sauce beneath. Serve warm or cold, with or without whipping cream.

Vera Swanson

ALISON'S EXCELLENT FRUIT PIZZA

1	20-ounce package Pillsbury's refrigerated sugar cookies
1	8-ounce package cream cheese, softened
1/3	cup sugar
1/2	teaspoon vanilla
	Banana slices
	Peeled kiwi slices
	Strawberry halves
	Blueberries
1/2	cup orange marmalade or peach or apricot preserves
2	tablespoons water

Freeze cookie dough for 1 hour. Slice into 1/8" thick slices. Line foil-lined 14" pizza pan with dough slices, overlapping edges slightly. Bake at 375° for 12 minutes or until golden brown; cool. Invert onto serving plate and carefully remove foil. Invert to right side. Combine cream cheese and vanilla; mixing well until blended. Spread over crust. Arrange fruit over cream cheese layer. Glaze with combined marmalade and water. Chill and cut into wedges for serving.

NOTE: Thin-sliced peaches, pears, apples and mandarin oranges also are nice. Add maraschino cherries and red or green grape halves for fun.

Barbara Molnar

APPLE BERRY SALSA

1	cup strawberries, chopped
1	kiwi fruit, chopped
1	Granny Smith apple, chopped
1	small orange, juiced
1	tablespoon grated orange zest
2	tablespoons brown sugar
1	tablespoon apple jelly
1	package flour tortillas
1	tablespoon sugar
1	teaspoon cinnamon

Combine fruit, orange juice and orange zest in a large mixing bowl. Add brown sugar and apple jelly. Mix well and chill for several hours.

TORTILLAS: Preheat oven to 475°. Mix 1 tablespoon sugar with 1 teaspoon cinnamon. Brush the tortillas with water. Sprinkle with the cinnamon/sugar mixture. Cut each tortilla into 8 wedges and place on a cookie sheet. Bake for 5 to 7 minutes until golden brown. Serve cool with salsa.

Barbara Helmus

Quotable Kid:

It's okay to lick your fingers, but not the knife.
Dylan, 5

LEMON CREAM MOLD

	Rind of 1/4 of a lemon, grated
1	envelope unflavored gelatin
3/4	cup sugar
	Pinch of salt
1 1/4	cups boiling water
2	egg whites, slightly beaten
2	tablespoons lemon juice
1	cup sour cream
1	cup heavy cream
	Strawberries, raspberries or peaches

Blend gelatin, sugar, salt and boiling water until gelatin dissolves. Chill until slightly thickened. Add egg whites, lemon juice and grated peel. Beat with electric mixer until fluffy; chill. When partially set, fold in sour cream. In covered container, blend heavy cream at low speed until just whipped. Fold whipped cream into lemon mixture. Spoon into 1/2-quart mold or 10 individual molds. Chill until firm, 6 hours or more. Unmold and serve with fresh fruit.

Nancy Gerhard

WARM BROWNIE PUDDING

2/3	cup sifted all-purpose flour
1/2	teaspoon baking powder
1/4	teaspoon salt
1/4	cup cocoa
2/3	cup broken walnut meats
2	eggs
2/3	cup soft butter
1	cup sugar
1	teaspoon vanilla
1	cup brown sugar, packed
6	tablespoons cocoa
2	cups hot water

Sift flour, baking powder, salt and 1/4 cup cocoa in mixing bowl. Add nuts and lightly mix in. Place eggs, butter, sugar and vanilla in glass container of electric blender. Cover container and turn on blender. Run until thoroughly blended, about 15 seconds. Pour blended mixture over sifted flour mixture and stir until just mixed. Spread evenly over bottom of a greased 8" square cake pan. Place brown sugar, 6 tablespoons cocoa and hot water in glass container of blender. Cover and blend 5 seconds. Pour evenly over batter in pan. Bake in 350° oven until pudding top has a brownie-like consistency, about 50 minutes.

Ann Williams

PINEAPPLE PUDDING
(FROM CHALMERS' GRANDMA)

1   large box instant vanilla pudding
1   8-ounce package cream cheese
1   8-ounce can crushed pineapple
3   cups milk

Soften cream cheese in microwave. Add 1 1/2 cups milk and mix with electric mixer or whisk. Add pudding and rest of milk; mix until smooth. Drain the pineapple and blend into mixture. Refrigerate until firm.

Helen Pierce

INDIAN TAPIOCA

3	tablespoons cornmeal
2	tablespoons sugar
1/8	teaspoon cinnamon
3	cups hot milk
3	tablespoons Minute Tapioca
1/2	teaspoon salt
1/2	teaspoon ginger
1/2	cup dark molasses

Combine cornmeal, Minute Tapioca, sugar, salt, cinnamon and ginger. Add hot milk and dark molasses. Stir well and pour into buttered baking dish. Bake at 325° for 45 minutes. Stir frequently while baking. Makes 6 servings.

June Holland

MATTHEW'S GRANDMOM'S KUGEL
(A.K.A. NOODLE PUDDING)

1	8-ounce package egg noodles, cooked according to directions
3	eggs
1/4	cup sugar
4	tablespoons butter, melted
1	teaspoon vanilla
1	quart low-fat buttermilk

Preheat oven to 350°. Place cooked noodles in 9x12" glass baking dish that has been lightly sprayed with cooking spray. Beat together remaining ingredients. Pour over noodles and carefully mix so that all noodles are well covered. Pat noodles gently down into liquid. The mixture will be *very* loose at this point. Bake for 40 minutes. Remove from oven and cover with crust made from:

1	cup corn flakes, crushed
1/2	cup finely chopped nuts (optional)
2	tablespoons brown sugar
1	teaspoon cinnamon

Bake an additional 20 minutes before serving to rave reviews!

Susan Wener

WHOOPIE PIES

Preheat oven to 350°.

2	eggs
2/3	cup shortening
2	cups sugar
2	cups milk
4	cups flour
1	cup cocoa
2	teaspoons baking soda
2	teaspoons vanilla
2	teaspoons salt

Mix dry ingredients together and add eggs, milk and vanilla. Drop onto cookie sheet by tablespoonsful and bake for 15 to 20 minutes; cool.

2	egg whites, beaten stiff
1/2	cup shortening
2	cups confectioners' sugar
1	teaspoon vanilla
1/2	teaspoon salt

Mix filling ingredients together and spread a teaspoon on one cookie, then top with another cookie to make a sandwich pie.

Tad Caldwell

BEST RUM CAKE EVER!

1 or 2	quarts rum
1	cup butter
1	teaspoon sugar
2	large eggs
1	cup dried fruit
	Baking powder
1	teaspoon baking soda
	Lemon juice
	Brown sugar
	Nuts

Before you start, sample the rum to check for quality. Good, isn't it? Now go ahead, select a large mixing bowl, measuring cup, etc. Check the rum again. It must be just right. To be sure the rum is of the highest quality, pour one level cup into a glass and rink it as fast as you can. With an electric mixer, beach one cup of butter in a fluffy bowl. Add to seaspoon of thugar and beat again. Meanwhile, make sure the rum is of the highest quality. Cry another tup. Open second quart if necessary. Add 2 large eggs, 2 cups fried druit and beat til high. If druit gets stuck in beater, just pry loose with a drewscriber. Sample the rum again, checking for tonscisticity. Next, sift 3 cups of pepper or salt (it really doesn't matter). Sample the rum again. Sift 1/2 pint of lemon juice. Fold in chopped butter and strained nuts. Add a babblespoon of brown thugar, or whatever color you can find. Wix well. Grease oven and turn cake pan to 350 gredees. Now pour the whole mess into the oven, and ake. Check the rum again, and bo to ged.

Tad Caldwell

MILE-HIGH BUTTERMILK CAKE

4	cups cake flour or 3 cups all-purpose flour
1	teaspoon baking soda
1/2	teaspoon baking powder
1	cup (2 sticks) butter, softened
3	cups sugar
1	teaspoon lemon extract
2	cups buttermilk
6	large egg whites

FILLING:

1	cup sugar
1/4	cup cornstarch
1/4	teaspoon salt
3	large egg yolks
1	tablespoons butter
4	teaspoons grated lemon peel
1/2	cup lemon juice

FROSTING:

1	cup milk
3	tablespoons all-purpose white flour
1	cup (2 sticks) butter, softened
1	cup sugar
	Lemon slices for garnish

CAKE; Preheat oven to 350°. Line three 9" round cake pans with waxed paper. In a medium bowl, stir together flour, baking soda and baking powder. In a large bowl, beat butter on high speed for 30 seconds. Add sugar and beat until fluffy. Beat in extract. Add flour mixture, alternately beating after each addition. Add egg whites; beat at medium speed for 2 minutes. Divide batter among prepared cake pans. Bake about 30 minutes until tops spring back when lightly pressed in the center. Cool in pans for 10 minutes; transfer cake layers to wire racks and let cool completely.

FILLING: In medium saucepan, over medium heat, combine sugar, cornstarch and salt. Gradually stir in 1 cup water. Cook and stir until thickened and bubbly; cook and stir 2 minutes longer. Place egg yolks in small bowl and gradually whisk in about half of the hot cornstarch mixture. Whisk this back into remaining cornstarch mixture; cook and stir 2 more minutes. Remove from heat; stir in butter and lemon peel. Stir in lemon juice. Cover with plastic wrap; let cool.

FROSTING: In small saucepan, whisk together milk and flour. Place over medium heat and cook and stir until thickened; cook and stir 1 minute longer. Cover with plastic wrap and cool. In a small bowl, beat butter for 30 seconds. Add sugar, beat until fluffy. Add cooled milk mixture; beat until fluffy. Reserve 1/4 cup of filling. Place one cake layer on serving plate. Spread with half of the filling. Add second cake layer; spread with the remaining filling. Add the third cake layer. Spread frosting over outside of cake. Drizzle top with reserved filling. Garnish with lemon slices.

Nancy Gerhard

PUMPKIN GINGER CHEESECAKE

Preheat oven to 350°.

GINGER CRUMB CRUST:

3	tablespoons butter
3/4	cup graham cracker crumbs
1/2	cup crushed gingersnaps
1	tablespoon brown sugar
1	teaspoon ground cinnamon

Place the butter in a small saucepan; melt over moderate heat. While the butter is melting, mix the graham cracker crumbs, gingersnaps, brown sugar and cinnamon in a medium bowl. Add the melted butter and mix with a fork. Press the crumb mixture into the bottom and sides of a 10" springform pan. Bake for 10 minutes, then remove from the oven and let cool. Reduce oven temperature to 300°.

FILLING:

1/2	cup heavy cream, chilled
1	3-ounce and 2 8-ounce packages cream cheese, softened
1	cup sugar
2	large eggs
1	cup cooked, mashed pumpkin, canned or fresh
1/2	teaspoon ground cinnamon
1/2	teaspoon powdered ginger
1/4	teaspoon ground cloves
1/4	cup pecan halves

To make the filling, pour the heavy cream into a medium bowl and beat just until soft peaks form; refrigerate. In a large bowl, beat the cream cheese with an electric mixer until fluffy. Gradually add the sugar, beating well. Add the eggs, one at a time and beat the mixture until it is fluffy, pale and homogenous. Stir in the pumpkin, cinnamon, ginger and cloves. Remove the whipped cream from the refrigerator and whisk lightly to reblend. Using a spatula or flat spoon, fold the whipped cream into the cream cheese-pumpkin mixture. Pour into the prepared crust and bake for 1 hour until firm. Cool the cheesecake to room temperature, then refrigerate for at least 3 hours before serving. Remove the sides of the springform pan. Just before serving place the pecan halves on top of the cheesecake.

Kimberly Smith

ORANGE NUT CAKE

6	eggs
2	cups sugar
2	cups ground pecans
2 1/2	sticks butter
1	cup plus flour
1	orange rind, grated

Blend eggs, butter, sugar, flour, pecans and orange rind. Pour into tube pan and bake at 350° for 1 hour. Cover with Orange Glaze.

ORANGE GLAZE:
Juice from 1 orange
Rind from 1 orange
1/2   cup sugar

Stir ingredients together until sugar is dissolved. Put on cake while still hot. Wrap in foil and let set overnight.

Marilyn Francis

GRAPEFRUIT CAKE AND FROSTING

1/4	cup butter, softened
1	tablespoon grapefruit rind, grated
3	eggs
1/2	cup water
3/4	teaspoon salt
1/4	teaspoon baking soda
1 1/2	cups sugar
1/2	teaspoon lemon rind, grated
1/2	cup grapefruit juice
3	cups cake flour
3 1/2	teaspoons baking powder

Cream together butter and sugar until light and fluffy; add rinds. Beat in eggs, one at a time. Blend well after each addition. Mix grapefruit juice and water together; set aside. Sift together flour, salt, baking powder and baking soda. Add sifted ingredients alternately with the juice-water combination to creamed mixture. (Use approximately 1/4 of the dry ingredients and 1/3 of the liquid ingredients each time.) Begin and end with the dry ingredients. Pour batter into 2 greased 9" round pans. Bake at 375° for 30 minutes or until browned and cake pulls away from sides of pan. Cool about 10 minutes. Invert on wire racks; cool. Put a thin layer of frosting between layers. Use remaining frosting for top and sides. Alternate sections of oranges and grapefruit for garnish.

FROSTING:

3	3-ounce packages cream cheese
4	teaspoons grapefruit rind, grated
1/4	teaspoon vanilla
1	tablespoon lemon juice
2	orange sections for garnish
1	grapefruit section (garnish)
1	tablespoon butter, softened
1	teaspoon orange rind, grated
6	cups powdered sugar, sifted
1	tablespoon orange juice

Soften cream cheese. Cream together cream cheese, butter, rinds and vanilla. Gradually add sugar and beat until smooth. Add lemon juice and orange juice gradually. Beat until frosting is at spread consistency.

Mrs. William LaMothe

CHOCOLATE ANGEL CAKE

1 1/2	cups egg whites
1	teaspoon cream of tartar
1/2	teaspoon salt
1	cup sugar
1	cup cake flour
1/2	cup cocoa
1	cup sugar

Beat stiff, but not dry: egg whites, cream of tartar and salt. Sift 1 cup sugar. Beat into egg whites until they make soft points (when you lift the beater, the tip of point just tips over). Sift together 3 times: 1 cup cake flour, 1/2 cup cocoa and 1 cup sugar. Fold carefully into egg mixture. Pour into 10" angel cake pan, dipped in cold water, and bake at 375° for about 35 minutes. Turn upside down to cool.

Jack Van Bell

Kitchen Tid-Bit:

When you need an instant cake decorator, put 1 cup of mini chocolate chips into a heavy-duty zipper-seal plastic bag. Set the bag in a bowl of hot water for about 5 minutes, or until the chips melt. Pat the bag dry with a towel and press the melted chocolate into one corner. With scissors, snip off a small piece (make sure it's small) of the corner where the chocolate is. Pipe away.

BETTER THAN RECESS CAKE

1	box yellow cake mix
1	box instant vanilla pudding
1/2	cup oil
1/2	cup water
1	6-ounce package Nestle's chocolate morsels
1	cake German chocolate, grated
1	8-ounce carton sour cream
4	eggs
1/2	cup chopped nuts (optional)

Combine all ingredients in mixer. Bake in tube pan at 350° for 55 minutes or until thoroughly done. Dust with sifted powdered sugar. Serve hot with cream or ice cream.

Boots Carter

APPLE CAKE

1 1/2	cups sugar
1	cup butter, melted
2	cups sifted flour
1	teaspoon soda
1	teaspoon cinnamon
1	cup chopped walnuts
2	eggs, beaten
1	teaspoon vanilla
2	teaspoons baking powder
1	teaspoon salt
3	cups chopped, unpeeled apples

Combine and mix sugar, eggs, butter and vanilla. Slowly add flour, baking powder, soda, salt and cinnamon. Add apples and walnuts. Pour into 9x13" pan. Bake at 350° for 60 minutes.

Sarah Stiener

A 19TH CENTURY ORANGE CAKE
(Mrs. D.A. Lincoln, 1887)

3/4	cup butter or shortening
1 1/2	cups sugar
3	eggs
1/2	cup orange juice
	Grated rind of 1 orange
2	tablespoons lemon juice
1/3	cup water
2 3/4	cups pastry flour
3 1/2	teaspoons baking powder
1	teaspoon salt
2	tablespoons melted butter
1	cup Cointreau
	Orange marmalade

Cream the butter and sugar until fluffy. Add the eggs, one at a time, beating briefly after each one, then the orange rind. Sift together the flour, baking powder and salt; combine orange juice and water, then add dry and wet ingredients, alternately to the batter. If you have used an electric mixer up to this point, complete the cake mixing. Pour into two 9" layer pans, greased and lined with waxed paper. Bake at 350° in a preheated oven for 25 to 30 minutes. Put the layers together with orange marmalade.

ORANGE ICING: Two cups confectioners' sugar diluted with warm orange juice and 2 tablespoons melted butter, until nearly the right consistency to spread. Add 1 tablespoon Cointreau, or more, until smooth and soft enough. Cool and frost the cake.

NOTE: Chocolate icing is terrific on this cake.

Molly Behrend

AUNT MARIE'S CHEESECAKE

2   8-ounce packages cream cheese
3   eggs
1   cup granulated sugar
1   pint sour cream
1   teaspoon vanilla extract

Preheat oven to 375°. Cream the cream cheese with mixer. Add sugar, eggs, sour cream and vanilla. Mix until well blended. Make a crust of:

1   cup graham cracker crumbs
1   tablespoon sugar
2   tablespoons butter, melted

Mix crust ingredients and press into a pie pan. Add the cream cheese mixture. Bake at 375° for 30 minutes. Turn off oven and leave the cheesecake in for 1 hour. Refrigerate before serving.

The Children's Education Center's Own
Miss Diane Barone

ORANGE CREAM CHEESE TART

PASTRY:
1	cup flour
1/4	pound butter
2	tablespoons confectioners' sugar

FILLING:
8	ounces cream cheese
1/2	cup sugar
2	tablespoons cream
2	tablespoons Grand Marnier
	Zest of 1 orange

TOPPING:
1	quart ripe red berries
1	cup currant jelly
1	tablespoon Kirsch

To make pastry, cut all in together. Press into 9 or 10" pie plate. Bake at 375° for 15 minutes.

Cream all filling ingredients together, layer in cooled crust; chill. Place berries on top.

Boil jelly until slightly thickened. Add Kirsch. Paint over fruit; chill.

Judy Starnes

RICOTTA CHEESE TART
WITH CORNMEAL CRUST

CRUST:

1/2	cup yellow cornmeal
3/4	cup all-purpose flour
1/2	teaspoon salt
3	tablespoons sugar
1/2	cup cold, unsalted butter, cut into pieces
1	large egg, lightly beaten

Combine the cornmeal, flour, salt and sugar; stir to mix. Add butter pieces and cut in with a pastry blender until the mixture is crumbly. Add beaten egg and stir until completely absorbed. Gather mixture into a ball, enclose in plastic wrap and refrigerate at least 1 hour.

FILLING:

1 1/2	cups ricotta cheese
1/2	cup granulated sugar
2	large eggs
2	teaspoons lemon zest
1/2	teaspoon vanilla
1/3	cup whipping cream
	Sifted confectioners' sugar for garnish

Beat ricotta and sugar until blended and smooth. Add the eggs and beat until fluffy. Stir in the lemon zest, vanilla and cream; mixing thoroughly. Roll out into an 11" round the soft pastry dough between 2 sheets of waxed paper that have been dusted with flour. Line a 9" tart pan with 1 1/2" sides with the dough. Pour in the cheese filling. Place the tart pan on a baking sheet and bake until filling is set, about 40 minutes. Cool on a wire rack. Dust the tart evenly with the sifted confectioners' sugar. Cut into wedges and serve at room temperature.

Cindy Pierce

NO-BAKE POLKA DOT PIE

Scoop balls of different flavored sorbets (passion fruit, mango, raspberry, etc.) using different sizes of ice cream scoops and melon ballers. Freeze on baking sheet for 3 to 4 hours. Soften one pint vanilla ice cream and spread into a pie pan lined with crushed vanilla wafers. Push half of the sorbet balls into ice cream and freeze. Top with another pint of softened vanilla ice cream; spreading to cover the sorbet balls. Top with small scoops of sorbet. Freeze again.

ICEBOX RASPBERRY COCONUT CREAM PIE

1	14-ounce can cream of coconut
1/3	cup sugar
1/4	cup water
1	1/4-ounce envelope gelatin
1 1/2	cups heavy cream
2	pints raspberries
1	graham cracker crust
	Raspberries and flaked coconut for garnish

Combine cream of coconut, sugar and water in small saucepan; sprinkle with gelatin. Dissolve over low heat and cool. Beat heavy cream and fold in coconut mixture. Add raspberries. Refrigerate until slightly firm. Press mixture into graham cracker crust; chill. Garnish with raspberries and flaked coconut before serving.

TEACHER'S ICE CREAM PIE

1/2	cup butter
1	cup brown sugar
3	cups corn flakes
1	cup coconut
1	cup chopped nuts
1/2	gallon vanilla ice cream, softened

Melt butter in saucepan. Add brown sugar and cook until dissolved. Continue to cook a few minutes longer. Mix in corn flakes, coconut and nuts. Pat 3/4 of this mixture into pie pan; fill with ice cream and top with remaining sugar mixture. Place in freezer immediately and freeze for at least 2 hours. To serve, top each slice with hot chocolate sauce.

The Children's Education Center's Own
Miss Lu Sares

PEACHES 'N' CREAM PIE

3/4	cup flour
1	teaspoon baking powder
1/2	teaspoon salt
1	egg
1/2	cup milk
3	tablespoons butter
1	3 1/4-ounce box vanilla pudding mix
1	15-ounce can sliced peaches, drained
8	ounces cream cheese
1/2	cup sugar
3	tablespoons juice from peaches
	Cinnamon

Preheat oven to 350°. Mix first 7 ingredients together and put in deep-dish pie pan. Spread peach slices over batter in pan. Mix together next 3 ingredients and spoon on top of peaches. Sprinkle with cinnamon. Bake for 30 to 35 minutes.

Liz Fowler

SANIBEL DISCOVERY PIE

CRUST:

2 1/2	cups graham cracker crumbs
1/2	cup sugar
1/2	cup butter or margarine

FILLING:

4	eggs, separated
1	can sweetened condensed milk
1/2	cup lime juice

CRUST: Melt butter, add crumbs and sugar; mix well. Reserve 1/2 cup. Divide remainder and press into 2 disposable pie tins. Bake at 350° for 10 minutes.

FILLING: In large mixer bowl, beat egg yolks until light and lemon colored. Add condensed milk; beat thoroughly. Beat in lime juice gradually. Beat egg whites until they form peaks; fold into egg mixture. Divide between the 2 pie shells. Sprinkle the top with reserved crumbs. Bake at 350° for 25 to 30 minutes.

NOTE: This has the consistency of cheesecake and the "discovery" is that one recipe of filling makes two 8" pies. If you have any crumbs left, refrigerate and use the next time.

Harriet Howe

PUMPKIN CHIFFON PIE

2	teaspoons unflavored gelatin
1/4	cup cold water
3	eggs, separated
1	cup sugar, divided
1 1/4	cups mashed, cooked pumpkin
1/2	teaspoon salt
1/2	teaspoon cinnamon
1/4	teaspoon nutmeg
1/2	teaspoon ginger
1/2	cup milk
1	baked pie crust (gingersnaps or plain)
	Whipping cream for topping

Soften gelatin in water for 5 minutes. Beat egg yolks. Add 1/2 cup sugar, pumpkin, salt, spices and milk. Cook over low heat, stirring constantly until mixture begins to thicken. Add gelatin in hot pumpkin and stir until dissolved; cool. When mixture begins to thicken, beat egg whites until almost stiff and beat in remaining sugar, one tablespoon at a time. Fold into pumpkin mixture. Pour into pie shell and chill until firm. Cover with whipped cream for topping if you wish.

Martha Ryckman
First director of The Children's Center

KEY LIME PIE

3/4	cup sugar
1/4	cup white Karo syrup
1/4	teaspoon salt
4	heaping tablespoons cornstarch
3	eggs, separated
1/2	cup Key lime juice
1 1/2	cups cold water
1	pie crust, regular or graham
6	tablespoons sugar

For pie, put cornstarch in pot. Add sugar, Karo, salt and the 3 egg yolks; stir and blend. Add 1 1/2 cups cold water and 1/2 cup lime juice; stir. Cook in double boiler until thick. Pour into crust. For meringue, beat 3 egg whites until stiff. Stir in gradually 6 tablespoons sugar and beat until sugar is dissolved. Spread on top of pie. Bake in 300° oven until golden brown, about 30 minutes.

TUNDRA MUD PIE

1 1/4	cups icebox chocolate wafers, finely crushed
1/4	cup soft or melted butter
	Coffee ice cream
	Chocolate fudge sauce

Roll chocolate cookies with rolling pin or put in blender to make fine crumbs. Melt margarine or butter and mix with crumbs. Press firmly in pie plate and freeze until firm. Soften ice cream and spread in cookie crust. Fill crust. Put in freezer to refreeze solid. Have chocolate fudge sauce at room temperature. You may warm slightly. Pour it on frozen pie until ice cream is covered; refreeze.

NOTE: This recipe is from McKinley National Park in Alaska!

Martha Ryckman
First director of the Children's Center

MANGO SHERBET

1	cup water
1/2	cup sugar
	Dash of salt
2	mangoes, peeled and sliced
1/2	cup light cream
1/4	cup lemon juice
2	egg whites
1/4	cup sugar

In saucepan, combine water, 1/2 cup sugar and salt. Cook 5 minutes; cool. In blender, puree mango with cream. Stir in cooled syrup and lemon juice. Freeze until partially frozen. Beat egg whites to soft peaks. Gradually add 1/4 cup sugar, beating to stiff peaks. Turn frozen mix into chilled bowl. Break into chunks. Beat until smooth. Fold in beaten egg whites. Return to freezer tray and freeze firm. Makes 6 to 8 servings.

Susie Santamaria

KEY LIME SHERBET

1	quart milk
2	cups sugar
1/2	cup Key lime juice
1	drop green food coloring

Dissolve the sugar in the milk. Add the key lime juice very slowly to the milk. It will become slightly thick in consistency. (Add 1 drop green food coloring to add just a blush of color.) Pour into freezer trays and freeze, stirring once when mixture begins firming. Garnish with slice of lime when served.

Shirley Evans

MORE, PLEASE!

*Proven Favorites for Discerning Young Diners
(including easy recipes for young
chefs to do themselves)*

TIPS FOR COOKING WITH KIDS

Give them their own cooking drawer, stocked with safe equipment. Include plastic dishes and bowls, a butter knife for spreading and cutting soft items, a wooden or plastic spoon for stirring, a wide pastry brush, colander, strainer and a roll of paper towels for spills.

Buy a sturdy, short stepping stool to help them reach counters and sinks. Never let children stand on barstools or chairs.

Give them their own squeeze bottles for soft or liquid items, such as ketchup, mayonnaise, mustard and honey.

An electric skillet is ideal for cooking with kids because you can set it up for them at an accessible level. Of course, you'll need to supervise at all times, and constantly remind young chefs that the pan is very hot.

Use bowls that are big enough to accommodate enthusiastic mixing!

The only knives children should ever use are serrated dinner knives and strong plastic picnic knives - and only with close supervision. Put a piece of colored masking tape on the handle and make the rule that hands must stay on the tape.

Putting things in and taking them out of the oven should be for grown-ups only.

Keep handles of pots and pans turned toward the back of the stove.

Have a sense of humor about the mess. Tell your kids that spills are what sponges are for.

Never, ever leave a child alone when cooking.

Have fun in the kitchen together!

TOASTED PUMPKIN SEEDS

    1   pumpkin
          Salt
          Water

Wash the seeds and remove the strings to the best of your ability. Let the seeds soak in salted water overnight (1 1/2 teaspoons salt per 2/3 cup water). Then place the seeds in a low baking pan in the oven at 300° for approximately 20 minutes or until golden. Eat with or without removing the shells.

Katie Anderson

COTTAGE CHEESE DIP

      Cottage cheese
      Milk
      Lemon or lime juice
1   pinch celery salt
1   pinch dried sage
1   pinch onion flakes or grated onion

Children make their individual servings in this recipe. Put 1 tablespoon cottage cheese in a cup. Add 1/2 teaspoon milk, 1/4 teaspoon lemon juice and the next 3 ingredients. Mix well with a spoon. Dip cut up vegetables or fruits or crackers in the mix.

                                        Children's Center

TUNA COTTAGE

1	7-ounce can chunky tuna
1	sweet pickle
1/2	cup cottage cheese
	Crackers or celery sticks

Open the can of tuna and put in medium bowl. Cut the pickle into tiny pieces with scissors. Put pieces in bowl. Put the cottage cheese in the bowl with the tuna and pickle; mix. Wash celery in cold water. Cut off the leaves. Put some Tuna Cottage on some celery sticks or crackers. Keep leftover Tuna Cottage in refrigerator.

Thana Loughney

HOLE-IN-ONE

Slices of bread
Butter
Eggs

Cut a hole in the middle of each slice of bread. Butter both sides of bread. Melt 1 tablespoon butter in a frying pan. Place the bread in the pan. Break the egg into a cup. Gently slide egg into the hole. Cook until firm, then turn and brown on the other side. An easy way to eat eggs and bread. The circles cut out are delicious buttered and browned in pan on both sides, too.

NOTE: You need Mom's help.

Mike Dunaway

CARROT PENNIES

2	large carrots, sliced into thin rounds
1	teaspoon butter (more or less)
3	shakes salt
1	squeeze lemon juice (from a small wedge)
1	teaspoon sesame seeds
1	tablespoon brown sugar (more or less)
1/4	cup water (more or less)

Have a grown-up slice the carrots and steam them until they're just tender. Add all the ingredients to a pan over medium heat. Cook and stir until the carrots are nicely coated with syrup. Add more sugar and/or water, depending on how syrupy you like it. Transfer to plates. Blow on it until it's comfortable to eat. Eat!

Cindy Pierce

ZUCCHINI MOONS

2   small zucchini
1   teaspoon butter (more or less)
2   tablespoons water
    A shake of salt
    A shake of pepper
2   teaspoons Parmesan cheese (or more
       to taste)

Cut the zucchini into rounds about 1/4" thick. Heat the pan to medium-hot. Put the zucchini, butter and water in the pan. Shake in some salt and pepper. Stir and cook until it seems done. This will take about 5 minutes. Sprinkle with cheese. (Kids love this part! And once the cheese is on they like to mix it up and smush it around before they settle down to eat it.) Eat! If it's too hot to eat right away, ask your child to count to 10 while you blow. If it's still too hot, trade jobs and do it again.

Cindy Pierce

JELLY MUFFINS

1	egg
1	cup milk
3	tablespoons butter, melted
2	cups flour
4	teaspoons baking powder
3	tablespoons sugar
1/2	teaspoon salt
	Jelly or jam

Beat the egg in a large bowl. Add milk and melted butter. Sift flour, baking powder, sugar and salt. Add to mixture in bowl. Mix well, but don't beat hard. Grease muffin tins and fill each about 1/3 full. Put 1/2 teaspoon jelly in each hole on top of batter. Cover with remaining batter. Bake for 25 minutes at 400°.

Christine Bowen

CHERRY RED APPLE SALAD

1-3   ounce can applesauce
1-3   ounce package cherry jello
1-6   ounce bottle 7-Up

Place applesauce in small saucepan. Heat over medium heat until bubbly hot. Add jello, stir until jello is dissolved. Set aside until cool. Stir in 7-Up; mix well. Pour into mold, chill until set.

Donna Sublett

CANDLE SALAD

1   lettuce leaf
1   canned pineapple ring
1   small banana
1   cherry

Rinse and drain lettuce leaf. Place on salad plate. Place pineapple slices on lettuce leaf. Cut banana flat on bottom to stand upright in pineapple hole. Place cherry on top of banana to make the flame using a toothpick to keep it in place.

NOTE: Don't forget to remove toothpick before eating your candle!

Donna Sublett

GREAT GREEN STUFF

1   small box pistachio pudding mix
16   ounces low-fat cottage cheese
1   can crushed pineapple
      Cool Whip to taste

Mix everything together in a great big bowl with a wooden spoon. Serve in individual bowls.

Maxine Fisher

MAKE-BELIEVE SOUP

2	cups orange juice
1/2	cup plain yogurt
1	tablespoon honey
2	teaspoons lemon juice
1	small banana, sliced
1	cup berries (any kind, fresh or frozen; if they're frozen, defrost them first, and use all the juice to add color to your soup)

Place the orange juice in a bowl. Add yogurt, honey and lemon juice; whisk until it's all one color. Get out 4 bowls. Place 5 bananas slices and 2 tablespoons berries in each bowl. Ladle the soup over the berries and bananas. Eat it up!

Cindy Pierce

FAT-FREE CARAMEL FRUIT DIP

8	ounces fat-free cream cheese
1/2	cup brown sugar
1	teaspoon vanilla

Blend everything in mixer. Serve with slices of apple and pear.

Maxine Fisher

CREAMSICLE FRUIT DIP

1   package instant vanilla pudding mix
1   cup milk
1/4 cup sour cream
1   can orange juice concentrate, right
      from freezer

Beat together pudding mix and milk. Add sour cream and orange juice concentrate and serve with fruit for dipping. (Jocelyn loves strawberries, melon chunks and banana slices!)

Lee Harder

COOL AND EASY GRAPES

White seedless grapes
Dark brown sugar
8 ounces plain yogurt

Fill glass bowl with white seedless grapes; chill. Pour 8 ounces plain yogurt over grapes; chill. Just before serving, sift dark brown sugar over top of yogurt. Must be served cold.

Leslie Goss

GRAPE CANDY

White or red seedless grapes

Rinse grapes and put in a plastic bag or Tupperware. Place in freezer and enjoy anytime right out of the freezer. Tastes like candy!

Katie Anderson

ORANGE BALLS

    60   round vanilla wafers
   1/4   cup orange juice
     4   teaspoons honey
         Sugar

Put 10 vanilla wafers in a plastic bag. Press the bag flat. Tie it closed. Whack the bag with a big spoon until all the wafers are tiny crumbs. Pour the crumbs into a bowl. Do this with all the wafers. Pour the orange juice into the bowl. Mix with a fork until it looks like wet sand. Put the honey in the bowl. Mix and mash with a fork until it sticks together. Pinch off a piece of the mixture. Roll it into a ball the size of a marble. Roll the ball in sugar. Let rest on plate for 10 minutes. Make all mixture into balls like this.

HAND COOKIES

2 2/3	cups margarine
3	cups sugar
2	teaspoons grated fresh lemon or orange peel
1	tablespoon vanilla
4	eggs
5	tablespoons plus 1 teaspoon milk
8	cups sifted flour
3	tablespoons baking powder
1	teaspoon salt

Cream shortening, sugar, peel and vanilla until smooth. Add eggs and milk; mix thoroughly. Sift and add dry ingredients. Chill in the refrigerator. Roll on floured surface until 1/4" thick. Trace around hands with fingers well spread. The children can use an ordinary blunt table knife; it has been the safest and most efficient tool. Sprinkle liberally with sugar and bake 7 to 9 minutes at 350° on greased cookie sheet.

Cindy Khemkhajon

FUDGESICLES

1	package chocolate pudding
1/2	cup sugar
3 1/2	cups milk
1/2	teaspoon vanilla

In a saucepan, cook to boiling, pudding, sugar and milk. (Use medium heat so the milk won't scorch.) Let the mix cool. Add the vanilla. Pour into paper cups. Place in freezer, when mushy, stick in spoons.

Suzanne Santamaria

BROWN SUGAR BUMPS

1/4   cup (1/2 stick) butter
1/2   cup brown sugar
1/4   cup peanut butter
1   cup oatmeal (regular or quick, but not instant)

Put the butter in a tea cup. Run some hot water from the faucet into the pan. Set the tea cup in the pan of hot water to melt the butter. If the water in the pan gets cool, pour it out and add more hot water. Stir the butter to help it melt. Pour the melted butter into a large bowl. Pack the 1/2 cup measure with brown sugar. Put the sugar in the bowl; mix. Mix in the peanut butter and then mix in the oatmeal. Put a spoonful of the cookie mix on a sheet of waxed paper. Gently pinch it to make it round. Do the same with the rest of the mix. Let the Brown Sugar Bumps rest for 15 minutes or more before eating.

NOTE: Chocolate Lumps may be made by substituting 1/2 cup instant sweet cocoa for the brown sugar.

Thana Loughney

WHITE CLOUDS AND FROSTING

Rice cakes
Cream cheese

Take one rice cake and spread with cream cheese. Makes one good, nutritious, light, after nap snack.

Katie Anderson

Notes

INDEX

WHAT'LL IT BE?

WE'LL DRINK TO THAT

SANIBEL STARTERS AND CAPTIVA CONDIMENTS

OUR DAILY BREAD

FROM SOUP TO SALAD

EAT YOUR VEGGIES

WHAT'S FOR SUPPER?

CATCH OF THE DAY

MEALS FOR THE MILLENNIUM

CASA YBEL COOKIES AND PERIWINKLE PIES

MORE, PLEASE

T hank you for purchasing this cookbook. We hope you will enjoy it for years to come. For almost 30 years, we've produced thousands of beautiful cookbooks for clubs, schools, churches, businesses, families and civic organizations. Have you ever considered putting one together for your own group or family?

All you have to do is collect recipes from your members and send them to us to be typed (or call for details for typing them yourself). We put them in book form with your choice of cover, dividers and extras. It's as easy as that! You can add history, hints and photos to personalize your book. Every recipe contributor gets credit in the book, making the project unique and meaningful. It's easy to be excited about something with that "personal touch".

Whether you are making money for your group or organization or making memories for your family, G & R can help you. Please call our toll free number or visit our website to receive our free information. Fundraising Has Never Been So Easy!!

To help you choose the Best Cookbook Company, take advantage of this special offer.

The Cookbook Specialists...
G & R Publishing Co.

507 Industrial Street
Waverly, IA 50677
1-800-383-1679

Publishing G & R Publishing G & R Publishing

G & R Publishing G & R

20¢
Off Per Book

Nieghborhood Delights

Club #1

The Cookbook Specialists...
G & R Publishing Co.
507 Industrial Street
Waverly, IA 50677

Toll Free 1-800-383-1679
www.cookbookprinting.com
email: gandr@gandrpublishing.com

Please submit this coupon with your completed order form for cookbooks.
This discount is not valid with any other special offer.

Good through
6/22/02

G & R Publishing G & R

Publishing G & R Publishing & R Publishing